At the age of nineteen, **Kenny McGovern** was diagnosed with what's known as 'Social Anxiety Disorder' and eventually became too ill to carry on working. As the years passed, he became almost housebound as a result of his illness and, as such, lost touch with many parts of life which although enjoyable are often taken for granted. Simple pleasures such as buying a nice sandwich from a local café or going out for a meal became impossible for him to do.

As a result of this, and because of his love of food and cooking, he eventually took to trying to recreate many of his favourite shop-bought foods at home. In 2010, Kenny decided to publish some selected recipes in his first book, *The Takeaway Secret: How to Cook Your Favourite Fast-Food at Home*, and it became an instant bestseller, following word-of-mouth recommendations on the internet.

With huge support and encouragement from readers, his confidence has grown, along with his food obsession. As a result, Kenny once more ventured into the world, researching and learning about the historic links between street food and local people and the recent upsurge in the modern, exciting and vibrant street food culture. His next book, *The Street Food Secret*, followed in 2017.

Over several visits to America, Kenny spent time observing the traditions and treats offered by American diner outlets to customers around the clock. As well as experiencing the delicious dishes on offer, he immediately became captivated by the atmosphere and community connection offered by local eateries. The value placed on the local diner cannot be overstated and the ethos is to be admired – honest cooking, delicious food and reasonable prices, accompanied by service with a smile! That was the inspiration beh'

THE AMERICAN DINER SECRET

How to Cook America's
Favourite Food at Home

Kenny McGovern

ROBINSON

ROBINSON

First published in Great Britain in 2019 by Robinson

1 3 5 7 9 10 8 6 4 2

A CIP catalogue record for this book
is available from the British Library.

ISBN: 978-1-47214-177-4

Typeset in New Caledonia by Hewer Text UK Ltd, Edinburgh
Printed and bound in Great Britain by Clays Ltd, Elcograf S.p.A.

Papers used by Robinson are from well-managed
forests and other responsible sources.

Robinson
An imprint of
Little, Brown Book Group
Carmelite House
50 Victoria Embankment
London EC4Y 0DZ

An Hachette UK Company
www.hachette.co.uk

www.littlebrown.co.uk

NOTES ON THE RECIPES

All eggs used in the book are large eggs.

All milk used in the book is whole milk/full-fat milk.

Where grated cheese is called for, it's always preferable to grate fresh as opposed to using shop-bought grated cheese. Pre-grated cheeses sold in shops often have cornflour or other ingredients added, which are designed to stop the cheese from gelling back together and results in a slightly drier texture than freshly grated cheese. That being said, of course, if pre-grated is all you have, go for it!

Dill pickles are available in a wide variety of forms in America – whole, sliced, chopped, spears, relish, etc. In the UK, our version of the same product is generally sold as 'gherkins' – look for dill amongst the ingredients and you'll know you're on the right track.

Oven temperatures relate to standard oven temperatures – for fan assisted ovens, cooking time should be reduced slightly, or cooking temperature lowered by 20°C.

Recipes may be scaled up or down as desired, providing quantity ratios remain consistent.

ACKNOWLEDGEMENTS

Thanks to Nikki Read and Giles Lewis at How To Books for continuing to support me in my food obsessions in this, my third book. Thanks to Jane Donovan for her exceptional editing skills and to Amanda Keats and all at Little, Brown for all their hard work and support.

To my fiancée, friends and family in Scotland, who show endless patience despite my progression from one food obsession to another. To Kirsty Bowker, for a uniquely Scottish opinion with a Philadelphia twist.

To my friends and family in America, whose hospitality and generosity made our visits so memorable. This book exists because of each and every one of you: James, Lois, Ian and Alex, Steve, Kerry, Sean, Rob, Lorie, Dave, Jesse. Here's to making more memories together.

To the diner chefs and restaurant staff of America, for waking up early and getting home late, prepping, cooking, cleaning and providing nutrition and comfort to millions of people across the country.

Always, ALWAYS, tip your server!

CONTENTS

2. SIDES & APPETISERS

3. SOUPS & SALADS

4. BURGERS, HOT DOGS & SANDWICHES

7. CONDIMENTS & ESSENTIALS

8. BAKER'S OVEN

9. DESSERTS & DRINKS

INTRODUCTION

Whether it's a group of young people socialising, a busy office worker grabbing lunch or a long-haul trucker stopping for food and a much-needed break, the American diner caters to all, often around the clock. Offering wholesome, family-style food at realistic prices, diner spots in America are an essential part of the history and culture of the United States.

An evolution of the 'lunch cart', a horse-drawn wagon that provided walk-up food service in the late 1800s, the American diner grew in popularity throughout the decades, despite some stumbling blocks along the way. Although initially suffering negatively from the effects of the Great Depression (1929–1939), the diner offered a comparatively inexpensive route into business for many, particularly in the northeast of the country. Later, with connectivity increased massively through the building of the highway system, customer numbers flourished as travellers made use of the convenience of a diner pit stop.

The diner also plays a huge part in the political history of the US, as demonstrated in the F. W. Woolworth lunch

1

counter sit-in (1960), an African-American protest which undoubtedly played a major role in bringing about change as part of the wider civil rights movement. The diner continues to play an important role in politics today, every politician or presidential candidate doing their utmost to visit their local diner for a photo opportunity, confirming, of course, that they're an 'average Joe' to potential voters.

The American diner is a beacon in the night for late-shift workers, a saving grace in the morning for hungover party people and an everyday spot for delicious dishes. It's an icon of American culture and looks set to continue to be so for many generations to come.

DINER-STYLE COOKING

In the vast majority of cases, diners are staffed by just a small number of cooks and servers, multi-talented and expected to turn their hand to a variety of chores. The diner chef is often tasked with preparing several different dishes at once and so must be adept at multitasking, with a high concentration level to match.

The business side of running a diner kitchen means preparation and frugality are also key; ensuring that dishes can be produced quickly means a fast turnover of diners, whilst smart use of leftovers ensures the business is profitable and food wastage kept to a minimum. Of course, as home cooks, these are all things we too aim to achieve in our kitchens, and so applying the skills and attitudes of a diner chef can be of benefit to us all.

Throughout the research for this book, I appreciated greatly the hard work and effort that diner staff put into making consistently delicious food, served up quickly and, hopefully, with a smile. I hope that with some of the recipes included, you'll be able to feed your guests classic American diner dishes.

Happy cooking!

Weight	
METRIC	IMPERIAL
25g	1oz
50g	2oz
75g	3oz
100g	4oz
150g	5oz
175g	6oz
200g	7oz
225g	8oz
250g	9oz
300g	10oz
350g	12oz
400g	14oz
450g	1lb

Oven temperatures	
CELSIUS	FAHRENHEIT
110°C	225°F
120°C	250°F
140°C	275°F
150°C	300°F
160°C	325°F
180°C	350°F
190°C	375°F
200°C	400°F
220°C	425°F
230°C	450°F
240°C	475°F

Liquids		
METRIC	IMPERIAL	US CUP
5ml	1 tsp	1 tsp
15ml	1 tbsp	1 tbsp
50ml	2fl oz	3 tbsp
60ml	2½fl oz	¼ cup
75ml	3fl oz	⅓ cup
100ml	4fl oz	scant ½ cup
125ml	4½ oz	½ cup
150ml	5fl oz	⅔ cup
200ml	7fl oz	scant 1 cup
250ml	9fl oz	1 cup
300ml	½ pint	1¼ cups
350ml	12fl oz	1⅓ cups
400ml	¾ pint	1¾ cups
500ml	17fl oz	2 cups

1

BREAKFAST

Many people believe breakfast is the most important meal of the day (I'm certainly one of them) and, when it comes to breakfast (and, to be accurate, lunch and brunch), the American diner is king. Savoury and sweet combinations of pancakes, French-toasted bread, waffles and biscuits combine with salty fried bacon, hunger-busting home fries, luxurious eggs and more. Of course, for a healthier option, fruit and yogurt-based alternatives are available.

One thing that makes a good diner is the all-day availability of breakfast dishes. With the following recipes, you'll be all set to cook up your breakfast and brunch favourites at any time of day. Just be sure to have plenty of softened butter and maple syrup on the side!

GRANOLA

Serves 6

Full of fruit and flavour! Once prepared, this will keep well in a lidded container in a cool, dry place for 7–10 days.

75g porridge (rolled) oats
15g cashew nuts, roughly chopped
1 tablespoon ground almonds
1 tablespoon sunflower seeds
1 tablespoon sesame seeds
2 teaspoons vegetable oil
2 tablespoons maple syrup
2 teaspoons honey
Dash of vanilla extract
2 tablespoons raisins
2 tablespoons dried coconut slices
Pinch of cinnamon
Fruit Parfait (page 8) or ice-cold milk, to serve

- Preheat the oven to 140°C/Gas 1. Meanwhile, in a large bowl, combine the porridge (rolled) oats, cashew nuts, almonds, sunflower seeds, sesame seeds, vegetable oil, maple syrup, honey and vanilla extract. Mix well.

- Tip the mixture out on to a baking tray and with a palette knife, spread it out to a single layer. Bake for 15 minutes.

Remove the tray from the oven, add the raisins, coconut slices and cinnamon. Mix well once more. Bake for a further 15 minutes.

- Remove the baked granola from the oven and set aside to cool for 2–3 minutes. Use a spatula to carefully transfer to a large bowl and allow to cool completely. Serve as part of a Fruit Parfait or simply with ice-cold milk.

FRUIT PARFAIT

Serves 1

You could use fresh fruit to make this parfait with good results. However, using frozen fruit and preparing the parfait ahead of time adds to the flavour as the fruit defrosts and the juices mingle with the yogurt and slightly soften the granola.

50ml Greek yogurt
1 teaspoon maple syrup or honey
50g frozen blueberries or mixed fruit
2 tablespoons Granola (page 6) or toasted porridge
    (rolled) oats
Pinch of cinnamon, to serve

- In a small bowl, combine the Greek yogurt and maple syrup or honey. Mix well.

- In a serving glass or bowl, layer as follows: yogurt mix, blueberries or mixed fruit, then Granola or toasted porridge (rolled) oats.

- Cover with plastic wrap and refrigerate overnight. Sprinkle with cinnamon just before serving.

PANCAKES

*Makes 12 large pancakes or 24 silver dollar pancakes**

Silver dollar pancakes are a uniquely American offering, smaller in size than regular pancakes and served in larger quantities. Blueberry Sauce (page 11), or maple syrup and butter are the perfect accompaniment.

240g self-raising flour
¼ teaspoon sea salt
60g caster sugar
2 eggs
300–350ml milk
A little vegetable oil

- Place the self-raising flour, sea salt and caster sugar in a large bowl. Mix well.

- Add the eggs and milk and mix well, adding more milk as necessary until a slightly thick batter is formed. Look for the consistency of double cream.

- Lightly grease a large heavy frying pan and set over a medium heat. When hot, pour a ladle of pancake batter into the pan and cook for around 1 minute or until bubbles form across the top of the pancake. Use a spatula to flip the pancake over.

- Cook the second side for a further 30–40 seconds, remove from the pan and keep warm in a clean tea towel. Repeat the process until all of the pancakes are cooked.

*For silver dollar pancakes, use just half a ladle of pancake batter at a time to form a larger number of smaller pancakes.

BLUEBERRY SAUCE

Serves 2

Serve over Waffles (page 19) or Pancakes (page 9).

125g blueberries (fresh or frozen)
1 tablespoon water
Pinch of cornflour
1 tablespoon caster sugar
½ teaspoon lemon juice

- In a large saucepan, combine the blueberries, water, corn-flour and caster sugar. Bring to the boil, reduce the heat to medium and simmer for 2 minutes, or until some of the blueberries have popped and the sauce is just beginning to thicken.

- Remove the pan from the heat, add the lemon juice and mix well. Allow to cool slightly before serving with Waffles or Pancakes.

CHOCOLATE-CHIP PANCAKES

Makes 6 pancakes

On one of many trips to Fisher's Cafe in New Jersey, these pancakes were impossible to resist. I knew as soon as they arrived at the table, this was one dish that simply *had* to be recreated!

120ml milk
Dash of lemon juice
1 egg
1 tablespoon melted butter
Dash of vanilla extract
150g plain flour
1 tablespoon cocoa powder
1 tablespoon caster sugar
1½ teaspoons baking powder
Pinch of cinnamon
Pinch of sea salt
3 tablespoons chocolate chips
A little vegetable oil
Sliced strawberries and Chocolate Syrup (page 271), to
    serve

• Combine the milk and lemon juice in a large jug. Mix briefly and set aside for 5 minutes. Add the egg, melted butter and vanilla extract. Mix once more.

- In a separate large bowl, combine the plain flour, cocoa powder, caster sugar, baking powder, cinnamon, sea salt and chocolate chips. Mix well.

- Combine the wet and dry ingredients in the bowl and mix until a batter is formed. Try not to over-mix the batter – a few lumps are OK.

- Heat a lightly greased heavy frying pan over a medium heat. When hot, pour a ladle of pancake mix into the pan at a time and fry for around 1–2 minutes or until bubbles form across the top of the pancake. Flip the pancake and cook for a further 30–40 seconds. Keep warm in a clean tea towel until all the pancakes are cooked.

- Serve the pancakes with sliced strawberries and Chocolate Syrup.

FRENCH TOAST

Serves 1

Crispy, fluffy French toast smothered in maple syrup is the perfect breakfast bread – particularly when sat alongside bacon, breakfast sausage and Home Fries (page 37)!

1 egg
3 tablespoons milk
¼ teaspoon cinnamon
½ teaspoon sea salt
½ teaspoon vanilla extract
Dash of maple syrup, plus extra to serve
2 slices bread (see Notes*)
1 tablespoon vegetable oil
1 tablespoon salted butter
1 teaspoon icing sugar
Maple syrup, to serve

- In a large shallow dish, combine the egg, milk, cinnamon, sea salt, vanilla extract and maple syrup. Mix well.

- Slice the bread into 8 triangles. Heat the vegetable oil and butter in a heavy frying pan set over a medium heat. Dip the bread triangles in the prepared batter, turning once or twice until fully coated. Carefully place in the hot pan and fry for 2–3 minutes on each side, or until crisp and golden.

- Remove the cooked French toast slices from the pan and arrange on a serving plate. If desired, keep warm on a rack in the oven at the lowest available temperature. Dust with sifted icing sugar and serve with maple syrup on the side.

Notes

Very fresh bread is not ideal for French toast as it soaks up too much of the egg mix and becomes soft and soggy. But there are various ways around this. Of course, slightly stale bread is ideal and a great way to use up bread a little past its best. Alternatively, leaving fresh bread on a rack for 1–2 hours to dry out a little will work, or you could dry the bread out in a low oven (140°C/Gas 1) for 20 minutes. Any of these methods will ensure that the French toast is fluffy on the inside with a nice crisp crust on the outside.

STUFFED FRENCH TOAST

Serves 1

You could also make this indulgent breakfast dish with thickly sliced fresh strawberries in place of the jam.

2 slices white, wholewheat or brioche bread (See Notes, page 15)
2 tablespoons cream cheese
2 tablespoons strawberry or raspberry jam
1 tablespoon vegetable oil
1 tablespoon salted butter
1 prepared French Toast batter (page 14)
1 teaspoon icing sugar
Maple syrup and fresh strawberries, to serve

- Spread each slice of bread with cream cheese and then strawberry or raspberry jam. Sandwich together.

- Heat the vegetable oil and butter in a heavy frying pan set over a medium heat. Dip the sandwich in the prepared batter, turning once or twice until fully coated. Carefully place the battered sandwich in the hot pan and fry for 2–3 minutes on each side, or until golden and crisp.

- Remove from the pan, slice into 2 triangles and arrange on a serving plate. Dust with sifted icing sugar and serve with maple syrup and fresh strawberries.

FRENCH TOAST STICKS

Serves 1

These bite-sized pieces of French toast, with their cinnamon-sugar dusting, are reminiscent of doughnuts – perfect for dunking in maple syrup.

2 thick slices white bread (See Notes, page 15)
1 egg
3 tablespoons milk
¼ teaspoon cinnamon
½ teaspoon sea salt
½ teaspoon vanilla extract
Dash of maple syrup, plus extra to serve
1 tablespoon vegetable oil
1 tablespoon salted butter
2 tablespoons Cinnamon Sugar (page 264)
Maple syrup, to serve

- Cut the bread slices into soldiers and set aside.

- In a large shallow dish, combine the egg, milk, cinnamon, sea salt, vanilla extract and maple syrup. Mix well.

- Heat the vegetable oil and butter in a heavy frying pan set over a medium heat. Dip the bread soldiers in the prepared batter, turning once or twice until fully coated. Carefully place in the hot pan and fry for 2–3 minutes on each side, or until crisp and golden.

- Remove the French Toast Sticks from the pan and arrange on a serving plate. Immediately dust with Cinnamon Sugar to coat evenly before serving with maple syrup.

WAFFLES

Makes 4 waffles (depending on the size/depth of your waffle iron)

A variety of waffle irons are widely available nowadays, many of them reasonably priced. If you don't want to eat all of the waffles straight away, cook them all regardless. Leftover waffles will store much more successfully once cooled (in a bread bin or tin) than the uncooked waffle batter. Reheat under the grill or in the toaster for 1–2 minutes.

120g plain flour
1 tablespoon caster sugar
2 teaspoons baking powder
¼ teaspoon sea salt
225ml milk
60g butter, melted
1 egg, separated
A little vegetable oil
Bacon and maple syrup, any fried chicken or Nashville
    Hot Chicken (page 73), to serve

- In a large bowl, combine the plain flour, caster sugar, baking powder and sea salt. Mix well.

- In a separate bowl or jug, combine the milk and melted butter. Mix well. Add the egg yolk to the milk and butter and mix well once more. Add the liquid mixture to the dry ingredients and mix until just combined.

- Whisk the egg white in a bowl until soft peaks form. Add the egg white to the waffle batter mix and gently stir through until just combined.

- Spoon the waffle batter into a lightly greased and preheated waffle iron and cook according to the manufacturer's instructions, usually around 5–7 minutes. If desired, the cooked waffles may be kept warm on a rack in the oven at the lowest available temperature whilst the remaining waffles are cooked.

- Serve your crispy waffles with bacon and maple syrup for breakfast, or with any fried chicken or Nashville Hot Chicken for a savoury-sweet diner classic! Any leftover waffles will freeze well (cover in plastic wrap) and can be toasted from frozen.

MULTI-GRAIN WAFFLES

Makes 4 waffles (depending on the size/depth of your waffle iron)

A tasty alternative to standard recipe waffles, made extra-delicious thanks to the addition of cinnamon and vanilla extract. Perfect with ice cream, fresh strawberries and Chocolate Syrup (page 271).

250ml milk
1 tablespoon lemon juice
2–4 tablespoons porridge (rolled) oats
1 egg
1 teaspoon melted butter
½ teaspoon vanilla extract
60g wholewheat plain flour
60g plain flour
1 tablespoon milled flaxseed
1 teaspoon chia seeds
1 teaspoon baking powder
Pinch of bicarbonate of soda
1 tablespoon soft brown sugar
1 teaspoon caster sugar
½ teaspoon cinnamon
A little vegetable oil

- In a large jug, combine the milk and lemon juice. Mix briefly and set aside for 5 minutes. Add the porridge (rolled) oats, mix again and set aside for 10 minutes. Add the egg, melted butter and vanilla extract. Mix once more.

- In a separate large bowl, combine the wholewheat flour, plain flour, milled flaxseed, chia seeds, baking powder, bicarbonate of soda, soft brown sugar, caster sugar and cinnamon. Mix well.

- Combine the wet and dry ingredients in the large bowl and mix until the batter has formed. Try not to overmix – a few lumps are OK.

- Spoon the waffle batter into your lightly greased and preheated waffle iron and cook according to the manufacturer's instructions, usually around 5–7 minutes. If desired, the cooked waffles may be kept warm on a rack in the oven at the lowest available temperature whilst the remaining waffles are cooked.

CHEDDAR-BACON WAFFLES

Makes 4 waffles (depending on the size/depth of your waffle iron)

These savoury waffles are almost tastier reheated in the toaster the next day!

200ml milk
1 teaspoon lemon juice
1 egg
1 teaspoon maple syrup
1 tablespoon melted butter
120g plain flour
1 teaspoon baking powder
Pinch of sea salt
Pinch of black pepper
4 slices of smoked streaky bacon, cooked and chopped
   (page 39)
50g mild or medium Cheddar cheese, grated
A little vegetable oil
Butter and maple syrup, or Hollandaise Sauce (page 31),
   to serve

- In a large jug, combine the milk and lemon juice. Mix briefly and set aside for 5 minutes. Add the egg, maple syrup and melted butter. Mix once more.

- In a separate large bowl, combine the plain flour, baking powder, sea salt and black pepper. Mix well. Add the cooked bacon pieces and grated cheese and mix once more.

- Combine the wet and dry ingredients and mix until a batter has formed. Try not to overmix – a few lumps are OK.

- Spoon the waffle batter into your lightly greased and preheated waffle iron and cook according to the manufacturer's instructions, usually around 5–7 minutes. If desired, the cooked waffles may be kept warm on a rack in the oven at the lowest available temperature whilst the remaining waffles are cooked.

- Serve with butter and maple syrup, or with Hollandaise Sauce.

EGGS

You can't make an omelette without breaking a few eggs, and you certainly can't make an American diner-style breakfast without doing the same. Eggs are at the very heart of the diner breakfast experience.

SUNNY SIDE UP

Serves 1

These eggs are cooked on one side only, resulting in a soft and runny yolk. Perfect with Breakfast Sausage and Home Fries (pages 40 and 37).

1 teaspoon vegetable oil
2 eggs
Pinch of sea salt
Pinch of black pepper
Finely sliced chives, to serve

- Heat the oil in a large frying pan set over a medium heat. When hot, tilt the pan to ensure the surface is coated in oil.

- Carefully crack the eggs into the pan and fry for around 2 minutes or until the whites have set, but the yolks are still soft.

- Carefully slide the cooked eggs on to a serving plate, season with salt and pepper and garnish with chives.

OVER EASY

Serves 1

'Over' refers to eggs flipped during cooking (or, alternatively, finished with water and a lid on top, as described below). 'Easy' means a soft yolk – occasionally, you'll find 'over medium' and 'over hard' options on a breakfast menu. Perfect with Breakfast Sausage and Hash Browns (pages 40 and 35).

  1 teaspoon vegetable oil
  2 eggs
  Pinch of sea salt
  Pinch of black pepper

- Cook the eggs as Sunny Side Up (page 26), but flip them over in the frying pan and cook for a further 20 seconds before serving.

- As an alternative to flipping the eggs in the frying pan, add 1 teaspoon water and immediately cover the pan with a lid. Cook for 20–30 seconds. The steam will slightly cook the top of the egg and give an 'over easy' finish.

- Season and serve.

SCRAMBLED EGGS

Serves 1

At the diner you can request your scrambled eggs to be 'soft scrambled' or 'hard scrambled' – the difference is simply cooking time, so adjust as necessary.

1½ teaspoons salted butter
2 eggs
Pinch of sea salt
Pinch of black pepper
Finely sliced chives, to serve

- Heat the butter in a saucepan set over a medium heat.

- As the butter heats, whisk the eggs vigorously in a bowl for around 30 seconds. When the butter has melted, add the eggs to the pan.

- Use a flat spatula to draw in the cooked egg from the sides of the pan every few seconds and cook the eggs for 2–3 minutes. When the eggs are almost cooked, turn off the heat and season with salt and pepper. Allow the residual heat to finish cooking the eggs for soft scrambled, or leave the heat on for about another 30 seconds for hard scrambled eggs.

- Slide the scrambled eggs on to a serving plate and garnish with sliced chives.

POACHED EGGS

Serves 1

The fresher the eggs, the better your poached eggs will be. I've used distilled white, malt and rice wine vinegars, all with good results.

2 drops vinegar
2 eggs
Pinch of sea salt
Pinch of black pepper
Finely sliced chives (optional), to serve

- Boil the water to cook the eggs in a large saucepan with the vinegar. Meanwhile, crack the eggs into individual small bowls or ramekins.

- When the water is boiling, use a wooden chopstick to stir until a small whirlpool is created. Carefully drop the eggs (not the bowls or ramekins) into the water.

- After 20 seconds, turn off the heat. Allow the eggs to continue cooking in the pan for around 4 minutes. Lift the poached eggs out of the pan with a slotted spoon, hold for 30 seconds (this allows the eggs to dry in their own heat) and arrange on a serving plate.

- Season and serve garnished with chives, if desired.

EGGS BENEDICT

Serves 1

The best part of a good Eggs Benedict experience is the combination of soft egg yolk and a smooth, indulgent Hollandaise. To ensure it all comes together perfectly, cook the bacon and toast your muffins first so that all your attention is focused on the eggs and sauce.

4 slices streaky bacon
1 shop-bought English muffin
2 Poached Eggs (page 29)
2 tablespoons Hollandaise Sauce (page 31)
Finely sliced chives, to serve

- Cook the bacon (page 39). Slice the English muffin in half and toast on both sides until golden.

- Arrange the muffin halves on a serving plate. Top with bacon, poached eggs and Hollandaise Sauce. Garnish with chives and serve.

Variation: For Eggs Royale, use smoked salmon (also known as 'lox') in place of the streaky bacon.

HOLLANDAISE SAUCE

Serves 1

In the two methods described below, a few drops of water may be added if the sauce begins to split or becomes too thick.

2 egg yolks
1½ teaspoons lemon juice
50g salted butter, melted
Pinch of sea salt
Pinch of cayenne pepper

- Fill a large saucepan one third full with water, bring to the boil and then reduce to a simmer.

- In a steel bowl, whisk the egg yolks and lemon juice until the mixture thickens. Place the bowl over the simmering water and slowly add the butter, whisking constantly until the mixture thickens and becomes smooth and glossy.

- Remove the sauce from the heat, add sea salt and cayenne pepper, mix once more and serve.

MICROWAVE METHOD

- Place the egg yolks and lemon juice in a microwavable bowl. Whisk thoroughly until the mixture thickens.

- Slowly add the melted butter, whisking until all of the butter is incorporated.

- Microwave the sauce for 10 seconds on full heat. Whisk thoroughly. Microwave for a further 10 seconds then whisk again. Season and serve.

DENVER OMELETTE

Serves 1

Originally known as a Western Omelette, the Denver is said to have been a popular dish amongst cowboys on long cattle drives.

1 teaspoon vegetable oil, plus extra for cooking
2 teaspoons salted butter
1 small onion, peeled and chopped
½ green pepper, deseeded and diced
½ red pepper, deseeded and diced
3 eggs
1 teaspoon water
Pinch of sea salt
Pinch of black pepper
3–4 slices cooked deli-style ham
1–2 cheese slices (Cheddar, Monterey Jack or processed)
Tomato ketchup (readymade or page 210) and Home
    Fries (page 37), to serve

- Heat the oil and butter in a heavy frying pan set over a medium heat. Add the chopped onion, green and red peppers. Stir-fry for 2–3 minutes, or until softened slightly. Remove the onion and peppers from the pan and set aside.

- Add the eggs, water, sea salt and black pepper to a large bowl. Whisk thoroughly. Ensure the pan is evenly coated with oil (add a little more, if it looks dry) and pour in the cooked egg mixture. Tilt the pan to ensure uncooked egg rolls around the whole pan. Add the cooked onion and peppers to one half of the egg mixture. Top with ham and cheese slices.

- Allow the omelette to cook for around 1 minute. Use a flat spatula to carefully lift it up from the untopped side (as the omelette is nearly cooked, it should become easier to lift from the pan). Fold over and continue cooking for 1 minute or until the cheese has melted.

- Slide the omelette on to a serving plate and serve with tomato ketchup and Home Fries.

HASH BROWNS

Serves 1

Crisp, salty, savoury potatoes are the perfect accompaniment to any breakfast. Hash browns take a few minutes to cook, but will happily look after themselves whilst you prepare your other favourite breakfast foods to serve alongside them. Perfect matched with Breakfast Sausage (page 40) or eggs (I like mine Over Easy, page 27).

1 large floury potato, peeled if desired (Maris Piper or
    King Edward are both good)
Pinch of garlic powder
Pinch of paprika
Pinch of sea salt
Pinch of black pepper
1 tablespoon vegetable oil
1 tablespoon salted butter
Over Easy eggs (page 27), to serve

• Grate the potato into a bowl of cold water and mix well. Rinse the cloudy water from the bowl, add more cold water and mix well once more. Drain well, squeezing as much water out of the grated potato with your hands as possible and pat dry on kitchen paper. Add the garlic powder, paprika, sea salt and black pepper to the potatoes and mix well.

- Heat the vegetable oil and butter in a heavy frying pan set over a medium heat. Arrange the grated potato over the surface of the pan, cover with a lid and fry for 5–6 minutes or until crispy on the bottom. Carefully flip and fry on the other side for a further 5–6 minutes or until golden and crispy.

- If desired, the cooked hash brown may be kept warm on a baking tray in the oven at the lowest available temperature.

HOME FRIES

Serves 1

The best home fries require a little forward planning but make life easy in the morning when it's time to prepare breakfast. They pair excellently with bacon, pancakes and your favourite eggs. Peel, if desired, or serve with the skin on for 'rustic' home fries.

1 large floury potato (Maris Piper or King Edward are both good)
1 tablespoon vegetable oil
1 tablespoon salted butter
Pinch of garlic powder
Pinch of paprika
Pinch of sea salt
Pinch of black pepper

- Cut the potato into bite-sized cubes and add to a large pan of water. Season generously with salt, bring to the boil and simmer for 5–6 minutes. Drain and set the potatoes aside to cool completely. Cover and refrigerate overnight.

- When ready to cook, heat the vegetable oil and butter in a heavy frying pan set over a medium heat. Add the potatoes to the pan and mix well to coat each piece of potato with oil.

THE AMERICAN DINER SECRET

Fry over a medium heat for 10–12 minutes, turning occasionally, until golden brown and crispy. When the potatoes are almost cooked, season with garlic powder, paprika, sea salt and black pepper.

BACON

Serves 1

When it comes to diner-style bacon, only streaky will do! Excellent with Pancakes or Waffles (pages 9 and 19), alongside some softened butter and maple syrup.

    1 teaspoon vegetable oil
    3 slices streaky bacon rashers, smoked or unsmoked
    1 teaspoon salted butter (optional)

- Heat a large heavy frying pan or griddle pan set over a medium-high heat. When hot, add the vegetable oil and tilt the pan until the surface is coated.

- Add the bacon rashers and fry for 2 minutes. Turn and fry for a further 2 minutes. For softer bacon with a little chew, remove from the pan now.

- For crispy bacon, cook the bacon for a further 1–2 minutes, turning once or twice more as necessary. Add the salted butter to the pan, drag each bacon slice through the melted butter and remove from the pan.

- The bacon will set a little and crisp up even more as it rests after cooking. Arrange the cooked bacon on a serving plate and serve with your favourite breakfast foods.

BREAKFAST SAUSAGE

Serves 4

Savoury homemade sausage with a hint of herbs and absolutely no preservatives! For a herbier sausage, increase the quantity of dried sage to 1 teaspoon. Any leftover sausage can be frozen after seasoning – simply defrost thoroughly in the refrigerator before use.

½–1 teaspoon dried sage
¼ teaspoon dried thyme
½ teaspoon dried parsley
Pinch of dried crushed chillies
¼ teaspoon coriander powder
Pinch of fennel
Pinch of nutmeg
¼ teaspoon dark soft brown sugar
1 teaspoon sea salt
¼ teaspoon black pepper
Pinch of white pepper
500g pork mince (not too lean, 15–20 per cent fat is ideal)
1 tablespoon olive oil
Pancakes or French Toast (pages 9 and 14) and eggs of
    your choice (pages 25)

- In a small bowl, combine the sage, thyme, parsley, chillies, coriander, fennel, nutmeg, sugar, sea salt, black and white peppers. Mix well.

- Place the pork mince in a large bowl. Add the prepared spice mixture and knead the spices into the meat until thoroughly combined. Let stand for 5 minutes before use, or cover in plastic wrap and freeze for up to 1 month at this stage, if desired.

- To cook the sausage: Heat 1 teaspoon olive oil in a heavy frying pan set over a medium-high heat. Drop small pieces of sausage mixture into the pan and fry, stirring only occasionally, for 3–4 minutes or until charred, crispy on the edges and cooked through.

- Alternatively, using wet hands, roll the sausage mixture into 10 meatballs, flatten on greaseproof paper and fry the patties in a large frying pan with a little heated oil set over a medium heat for 2–3 minutes each side or until well browned and cooked through.

- Serve with Pancakes or French Toast and eggs.

CORNED BEEF HASH

Serves 1

The potato may be peeled, if desired, or left skin-on for 'rustic' hash.

 1 large floury potato, peeled or unpeeled (Maris Piper or
   King Edward are both good)
 1 teaspoon vegetable oil
 1 teaspoon salted butter
 1 small onion, peeled and finely chopped
 3 slices deli-style corned beef (around 90g), roughly
   chopped
 1 teaspoon Worcestershire sauce
 Pinch of garlic powder
 Pinch of sea salt
 Pinch of black pepper
 Poached Egg (page 29) and tomato ketchup (readymade
   or page 210), if desired, to serve

- Cut the potato into small bite-sized cubes and add to a large pan of water. Season generously with salt, bring to the boil and simmer for 5 minutes. Drain the potatoes and set aside to cool.

- When ready to cook, heat the vegetable oil and butter in a heavy frying pan set over a medium heat. Add the onion to the pan and stir-fry for 3–4 minutes. Add the potatoes and mix well to coat with oil. Fry for 7–8 minutes, stirring occasionally.

- Add the corned beef, Worcestershire sauce, garlic powder, sea salt and black pepper. Mix well, pressing the mixture down across the surface of the pan with a spatula, and fry for a further 8–10 minutes over a medium-high heat. As the hash cooks, allow it to brown, untouched, for a minute or two at a time before turning to ensure the browned/crispy pieces from the base of the pan are mixed through.

- When the corned beef hash is as golden and crispy as you like it, slide it on to a serving plate. Top with a Poached Egg and serve immediately with tomato ketchup on the side, if desired.

BISCUITS

Makes 4 biscuits

This recipe has its origins in the Deep South, an area with strong historic Scottish connections. It's probably no coincidence that the savoury-sweet biscuits, with their buttery crumb, resemble both Scottish shortbread and traditional scones. They go perfectly with Nashville Hot Chicken or Chicken Fingers (pages 73 and 67), or slice in half and top generously with Sausage Gravy (page 232).

125g plain flour, plus extra for rolling out
1½ teaspoons baking powder
1½ teaspoons caster sugar
Pinch of sea salt
75ml milk, plus extra for brushing
½ teaspoon lemon juice
50g salted butter (frozen for around 1 hour until solid)
Vegetable oil for greasing

• Preheat the oven to 200°C/Gas 6. In a large bowl, combine the plain flour, baking powder, caster sugar and sea salt. Mix well. In a small cup, combine the milk and lemon juice and set aside for 5 minutes.

• Grate the frozen butter into the flour mixture and toss together. Add the wet ingredients and stir to form a dough.

Empty the dough out on to a floured work surface and draw together with your hands. Lightly pat or roll out to a thickness of around 3.5cm. For a flakier, layered biscuit, roll the dough thinner, fold it in two and roll out again. Repeat this process two to three times to create layers in the dough. Alternatively, simply proceed from the point of having rolled the dough out to a thickness of 3.5cm.

- Use a round cutter to cut the dough into 3 biscuits (avoid twisting the cutter as this will prevent rising).

- Lightly grease a baking tray. With a palette knife, lift the prepared biscuits on to the baking tray, brush with a little milk and bake for 12–15 minutes or until golden. Transfer to a wire rack to crisp up.

Note: Any leftover biscuits may be split and toasted later on in the day with reasonable results, but they're so good fresh from the oven that you'll always favour making a new batch!

HUEVOS RANCHEROS

Serves 1

1 tablespoon vegetable oil
2 x 12cm readymade soft corn tortillas
2 eggs, sunny side up (page 26)
2 tablespoons tinned refried beans
Handful fresh coriander leaves, finely chopped

Tomato-chilli Sauce
1 teaspoon vegetable oil
2 plum tomatoes from a tin
1 garlic clove, peeled and crushed
1 jalapeño chilli, deseeded and sliced
Pinch of cumin powder
Pinch of dried oregano
Pinch of sea salt
Pinch of black pepper

- First, make the Tomato-chilli Sauce. Heat the oil in a large frying pan set over a medium heat. Add the plum tomatoes, garlic and chilli. Fry for 1 minute. Add the cumin powder, oregano, sea salt and black pepper. Mix well and cook for a further minute.

- Mash the sauce, or blend until completely smooth as desired. Set aside and keep warm.

- To make the huevos rancheros, heat the vegetable oil in a large frying pan set over a medium heat. Add the tortillas and fry for around 10–15 seconds on each side. Drain off any excess oil and arrange the tortillas on a serving plate.

- Add the eggs to the frying pan and cook for around 2 minutes, basting with oil from the pan as they cook. Meanwhile, warm the beans.

- Top the corn tortillas with refried beans. Add the fried eggs, top with sauce and serve garnished with fresh coriander leaves.

BREAKFAST TACOS

Serves 1

It's worth sourcing proper soft corn tortillas, if possible –
many supermarket brands of tortillas include a quantity of
wheat flour, which is a different experience altogether.

This simple spicy breakfast is a delicious morning eye-
opener. You could, of course, add Bacon, Pulled Pork or
Breakfast Sausage (pages 39, 184 and 40).

3 x 12cm readymade soft corn tortillas
1 portion Scrambled Eggs (page 28)
3 teaspoons mayonnaise
1–2 tablespoons Fresh Tomato Salsa (page 214)
Sriracha sauce (widely available in supermarkets and
    online) or Sriracha Mayo (page 221), to serve

- Heat a large dry frying pan set over a medium heat. Once
  hot, add the tortillas and toast for around 30–40 seconds.
  Flip with a spatula and toast for a further 30–40 seconds.
  Set aside in a warming basket or cover with a clean dry
  cloth to keep warm whilst you cook the eggs.

- To serve, spread 1 teaspoon mayonnaise on each tortilla.
  Top with Scrambled Eggs and Fresh Tomato Salsa. Finish
  with Sriracha sauce or Sriracha Mayo and serve.

2

SIDES & APPETISERS

The versatility of diner menus means a lack of choice is never an issue. In fact, choosing just one dish from a menu where each sounds more delicious than the next can prove tricky indeed!

When variety is the spice of life, side dishes and appetisers is the only way to go. A selection of smaller plates, shared amongst friends ('we'll take an order of those for the table . . .') – this chapter is dedicated to those baskets and platters that just have to be ordered. Ribs, wings, nachos, onion rings . . . the dishes you don't really need, but you just have to have!

ONION RINGS

Serves 2

1 large Spanish onion
175g plain flour
1 teaspoon baking powder
1 teaspoon sea salt
1 egg
175ml milk
1 teaspoon Frank's Red Hot Sauce
125g Panko breadcrumbs
Pinch of cayenne pepper
Pinch of garlic powder
Pinch of black pepper
Vegetable oil for deep-frying
A little sea salt or Cajun Seasoning (page 228), to serve

- First, peel the onion and slice into rings about 1cm in diameter.

- Place the plain flour, baking powder and sea salt in a large bowl. Mix well.

- In a separate bowl, combine the egg, milk and hot sauce, whisking until smooth.

- Add the Panko breadcrumbs, cayenne pepper, garlic powder and black pepper to another bowl. Mix well.

- Keeping one hand dry, dip the onion rings first in the flour, then in the wet mixture, and finally, into the seasoned Panko breadcrumbs, shaking off any excess.

- Heat the oil for deep-frying to 180°C/350°F. Carefully place the breaded onion rings in the hot oil and fry for 2–3 minutes or until golden and crispy. Remove from the pan, place on kitchen paper to drain off any excess oil and then arrange on a serving plate. Season with a little sea salt or Cajun Seasoning and serve.

SHOESTRING ONIONS

Serves 4

250ml milk
1 tablespoon lemon juice
2 large onions, peeled and thinly sliced
8 tablespoons plain flour
¼ teaspoon garlic powder
Pinch of cayenne pepper
1 teaspoon sea salt, plus extra for seasoning
½ teaspoon black pepper
Vegetable oil for deep-frying
Cajun Seasoning (page 228, optional)

- Place the milk and lemon juice in a large shallow dish. Mix briefly and set aside for 5 minutes. Add the sliced onions and mix well until all of the onions are covered. Set aside to soak for around 1 hour.

- Place the plain flour, garlic powder, cayenne pepper, sea salt and black pepper in a large bowl. Mix well.

- Heat the oil for deep-frying to 180°C/350°F. Drain the onions through a sieve and add to the seasoned flour; mix well. When the oil is hot, lift a handful of breaded onions from the bowl, shaking off any excess flour, and place carefully in the hot oil. Fry for 2–3 minutes or until golden and crispy.

- Remove the fried onions from the pan, drain off any excess oil and transfer to a kitchen paper-lined plate. Season with extra sea salt whilst the onions are still piping hot (alternatively, season with Cajun Seasoning).

- Repeat the process until all of the onions are fried. Serve whilst hot, or allow to cool completely and then store in a sealed container in a cool, dry place for 2–3 days. Serve as a snack or on top of a Smashed Burger (page 120).

GARLIC-CHEESE MUSHROOMS

Serves 1–2

The crusty bread is an essential accompaniment to this dish to ensure not a drop of the delicious sauce is wasted!

250g chestnut mushrooms
1 teaspoon vegetable oil
1 teaspoon salted butter
½ small onion, peeled and finely chopped
2 garlic cloves, peeled and crushed
75ml double cream
75ml milk
½ teaspoon cornflour
1–2 tablespoons grated Parmesan cheese
Pinch of sea salt
Pinch of black pepper
Pinch of dried parsley
Country Bread (page 236), to serve

- Wipe the mushrooms clean with kitchen paper and cut into halves or quarters depending on size (leave quite chunky).

- Heat the vegetable oil and butter in a large frying pan set over a high heat. Add the mushrooms and fry for 2–3 minutes, stirring occasionally. Reduce the heat to low. Add the chopped onion and fry for 2 minutes. Add the crushed garlic and fry for a further minute.

- Stir in the double cream. Mix the milk and cornflour together in a jug and add to the pan, stirring to combine with the cream. Add the grated Parmesan cheese, sea salt, black pepper and dried parsley.

- Cook the sauce for 1–2 minutes, stirring often, until thick and smooth. Transfer the mushrooms to a serving bowl and serve with Country Bread.

MOZZARELLA STICKS

Serves 2

4 tablespoons plain flour
4 tablespoons Panko breadcrumbs
¼ teaspoon garlic powder
¼ teaspoon onion powder
Pinch of dried Italian herbs
Pinch of cayenne pepper
¼ teaspoon sea salt
¼ teaspoon black pepper
1 egg
3 tablespoons milk
1 teaspoon Frank's Red Hot Sauce
125g mozzarella, cut into sticks
Vegetable oil for deep-frying
Marinara Sauce (page 175), to serve

- Place the plain flour, Panko breadcrumbs, garlic powder, onion powder, Italian herbs, cayenne pepper, sea salt and black pepper in a large bowl. Mix well and tip on to a large plate.

- Place the egg, milk and hot sauce in another large bowl; mix well.

- Keeping one hand dry and working one stick at a time, dip each mozzarella stick in the egg mix, then into the seasoned breadcrumbs. Dip the mozzarella sticks back in the egg once more and finally, into the seasoned breadcrumbs to form a double breading.

- Repeat this process with each mozzarella strip and arrange the breaded strips on a plate. At this stage the mozzarella sticks can be covered and set aside in the refrigerator for several hours before frying, if desired.

- Heat the oil for deep-frying to 180°C/350°F. Carefully place each mozzarella stick in the hot oil and fry for around 2 minutes, turning occasionally until the breading is golden and crispy. Remove from the pan, drain off any excess oil on kitchen paper and arrange on a serving plate. Serve with Marinara Sauce.

SPINACH & ARTICHOKE DIP

Serves 2–4

150g fresh spinach leaves
1 garlic clove, peeled and crushed
400g tin artichoke hearts, drained and finely chopped
75g sour cream
75g mayonnaise
2 tablespoons single cream
75g grated Parmesan cheese
Handful grated mozzarella cheese
1 teaspoon hot sauce (I used Frank's Red Hot Sauce)
¼ teaspoon garlic powder
¼ teaspoon onion powder
¼ teaspoon sea salt
¼ teaspoon black pepper
Tortilla Chips (page 62), to serve

- Bring a large pan of water to the boil. Add the fresh spinach leaves, mix well and leave in the pan for 1 minute. Drain the spinach, rinse briefly in cold water until cool enough to handle and squeeze out as much water as you can. The large quantity of spinach will reduce to not much more than a handful of leaves and will turn an intense green.

- Roughly chop the prepared spinach and place in a large bowl. Add the crushed garlic, chopped artichoke hearts, sour cream, mayonnaise, single cream, Parmesan cheese, mozzarella cheese, hot sauce, garlic powder, onion powder, sea salt and black pepper. Mix well.

- Preheat the oven to 180°C/Gas 4. Pour the prepared dip into one large roasting dish, or into individual ramekins, if desired. Place the dish/ramekins on a baking tray and bake for 20–25 minutes in the centre of the oven. Remove the baked dip from the oven and serve with Tortilla Chips.

CHILLI-CHEESE DIP

Serves 1–2

4 tablespoons mayonnaise
4 tablespoons sour cream
2 tablespoons milk, plus extra as necessary
30g grated Cheddar cheese
1 slice Monterey Jack cheese
5–6 pickled jalapeños, finely chopped
Pinch of cayenne pepper
Pinch of sea salt
Pinch of black pepper
Tortilla Chips (page 62), to serve

- Place the mayonnaise, sour cream and milk in a large saucepan. Warm over a low heat until combined. Add the Cheddar and Monterey Jack cheeses. Cook for a further 2–3 minutes or until the cheese has melted and the sauce is slightly thick. Add more milk as necessary if the sauce thickens too quickly.

- Add the chopped jalapeños, cayenne pepper, sea salt and black pepper; mix well. Pour the sauce into a serving bowl and serve immediately with Tortilla Chips.

Variation: Alternatively, for a slightly crispy topping, pour the sauce into a baking dish, top with a little extra cheese and bake in a hot oven (180°C/Gas 4) for 3–4 minutes.

TORTILLA CHIPS

Serves 1

Both flour and soft corn tortillas can be used to make chips, with slightly different, but equally delicious results.

> 4 small soft corn or wheat flour tortillas
> Vegetable oil for deep-frying
> Sea salt, to taste

- With kitchen scissors, cut each corn tortilla in half. Cut each half into thirds to create 6 triangular tortilla chips per tortilla.

- Heat the oil to around 180°C/350°F. Fry the tortilla chips in batches for around 2–3 minutes, or until golden and crispy. As the chips cook, drain off any excess oil and arrange on a plate lined with kitchen paper. Season to taste with sea salt whilst still warm.

PIMENTO CHEESE

Serves 1

Delicious as a grilled cheese sandwich filling or even served simply with Tortilla Chips (page 62), you could spice this up by adding chopped jalapeños or dried crushed chilli flakes, if desired.

40g grated medium Cheddar cheese
1 tablespoon soft cream cheese
2 tablespoons mayonnaise
½ teaspoon yellow (American) mustard
2 tablespoons roasted red peppers from a jar, deseeded and finely chopped
Pinch of garlic powder
Pinch of onion powder
Pinch of cayenne pepper
Pinch of sea salt
Pinch of black pepper
Pinch of white pepper

- Place all the ingredients in a large bowl. Mix thoroughly until well combined. Cover and set aside in the refrigerator for at least 1 hour before use.

- The Pimento Cheese will keep well in the refrigerator for up to 3 days.

NACHOS

Serves 1

Large handful corn tortilla chips (make your own, page
  62)
3 tablespoons Chilli (page 195)
1 tablespoon tinned refried beans (optional)
1 salad tomato, skinned, deseeded and diced
1 spring onion, trimmed, peeled and finely sliced
Large handful grated Cheddar cheese
Large handful grated mozzarella cheese
Small handful fresh coriander leaves, finely chopped
Sour cream, guacamole and Fresh Tomato Salsa (page
  214), to serve

- Preheat the oven to 200°C/Gas 6. Arrange half of the
  tortilla chips on a large roasting tray. Top with half of the
  Chilli, refried beans, tomato, spring onion, Cheddar and
  mozzarella cheeses.

- Add the remaining tortilla chips and top with the remaining Chilli, refried beans, tomato, spring onion, Cheddar
  and mozzarella cheese. Bake in the centre of the oven for
  10–15 minutes, or until the cheese has melted and the
  nachos are crunchy.

- Remove the nachos from the oven. Garnish with fresh coriander, sour cream, guacamole and Fresh Tomato Salsa.

BREADED KING PRAWNS

Serves 1–2

100g plain flour
¼ teaspoon garlic powder
¼ teaspoon onion powder
¼ teaspoon dried Italian herbs (optional)
¼ teaspoon sea salt
¼ teaspoon black pepper
1 egg
3 tablespoons milk
1 teaspoon Frank's Red Hot Sauce
10–12 large raw King prawns
Vegetable oil for deep-frying
Remoulade or Tartare Sauce, to serve (pages 219 and 218)

- To a large bowl, add the plain flour, garlic powder, onion powder, Italian herbs (if desired), sea salt and black pepper. Mix well and tip on to a large plate.

- Add the egg, milk and hot sauce to a large bowl; mix well.

- Keeping one hand dry and working one at a time, dip each King prawn in egg, then in the seasoned flour. Dip in egg once more and finally in the seasoned flour to form a double breading. Repeat this process with each prawn and arrange on a plate. At this stage the breaded prawns can be covered and set aside in the refrigerator for 1–2 hours before frying, if desired.

- Heat the oil for deep-frying to 180°C/350°F. Carefully place each breaded prawn in the hot oil and fry for 2–3 minutes, turning occasionally, until the prawns are cooked and the breading is golden and crispy. Remove from the pan, drain off any excess oil on kitchen paper and arrange on a serving plate. Serve with Remoulade or Tartare Sauce.

CHICKEN FINGERS

Serves 1–2

100g plain flour
¼ teaspoon garlic powder
¼ teaspoon onion powder
¼ teaspoon dried Italian herbs (optional)
¼ teaspoon sea salt
¼ teaspoon black pepper
1 egg
3 tablespoons milk
1 teaspoon Frank's Red Hot Sauce
1 skinless, boneless chicken breast fillet (125g)
Vegetable oil for deep-frying
Honey Mustard Dip (page 224), Sweet BBQ Sauce (page 215), Ranch Dressing (page 217) and celery sticks, to serve

- Place the plain flour, garlic powder, onion powder, Italian herbs (if desired), sea salt and black pepper in a large bowl. Mix well and transfer to a large plate.

- To a large bowl, add the egg, milk and hot sauce. Mix well.

- With kitchen scissors, cut the chicken breast into 5–6 long strips. Keeping one hand dry and working one strip at a time, dip each chicken strip in the egg mix, then in the seasoned flour. Dip the chicken strip back in the egg mix once more and finally, in the seasoned flour to form a double breading.

- Repeat this process with each chicken strip and arrange the breaded strips on a plate. At this stage the strips can be covered and set aside in the refrigerator for several hours before frying, if desired.

- Heat the oil for deep-frying to 180°C/350°F. Carefully place each chicken strip in the hot oil and fry for 4–5 minutes, turning occasionally. Fry until nicely golden brown and crispy. (If you're unsure, use a temperature probe to ensure the chicken has reached an internal temperature of over 75°C/167°F.)

- Remove the chicken strips from the pan, drain off any excess oil on kitchen paper and arrange on a serving plate. Serve with Honey Mustard Dip, Sweet BBQ Sauce, Ranch Dressing and celery sticks.

MAPLE BUFFALO WINGS

Serves 1–2

These spicy, slightly sweet chicken wings are deliciously addictive!

100g plain flour
½ teaspoon garlic powder
1 teaspoon paprika
¼ teaspoon sea salt
¼ teaspoon black pepper
Vegetable oil for deep-frying
1kg chicken wings, split into wing pieces, tips removed
4 tablespoons Frank's Red Hot Sauce
4 tablespoons salted butter
Pinch of garlic powder
1 tablespoon maple syrup
Ranch Dressing (page 215) and celery sticks, to serve

- Place the plain flour, garlic powder, paprika, sea salt and black pepper in a bowl. Mix well, then spread out on a large plate.

- Heat the oil for deep-frying to 180°C/350°F. Press each chicken wing piece in the seasoned flour, shaking off any excess. Carefully place each wing in the hot oil. Fry in batches to avoid overcrowding the pan.

- Fry the wings for 15 minutes, turning occasionally, until nicely brown and crispy. (If you're unsure, use a temperature probe to ensure the wings have reached an internal temperature of over 75°C/167°F.) Remove from the pan, drain off any excess oil on kitchen paper and place in a large bowl.

- In a small saucepan, place Frank's Red Hot Sauce, salted butter, garlic powder and maple syrup. Mix well over a medium heat until the butter has melted and the sauce is piping hot.

- Pour the prepared sauce over the fried wings and toss to coat. Arrange the Maple Buffalo Wings on a serving plate and serve with Ranch Dressing and celery sticks.

CRISPY CHICKEN WINGS

Makes around 24 wings

This simple marinade and breading produces perfect crispy wings every time! Delicious served with Sweet BBQ Sauce (page 215).

1kg chicken wings, jointed and wing tips removed
½ teaspoon sea salt, plus extra to serve
½ teaspoon black pepper
½ teaspoon Chinese five-spice
Vegetable oil for deep-frying
1 egg, beaten
150g plain flour
Your favourite wing sauce, to serve (optional)

- Place the chicken wings, sea salt, black pepper and Chinese five-spice in a large bowl. Mix thoroughly, cover with plastic wrap and set aside in the refrigerator for 2 hours.

- Heat the oil for deep-frying to 180°C/350°F. Meanwhile, add the egg to the marinated chicken wings and mix thoroughly. Put the plain flour in a separate large bowl and press each marinated chicken wing into the flour until thoroughly coated.

- Fry the wings in two batches to ensure the pan isn't overcrowded. When the oil is hot, carefully place the breaded chicken wings in the hot oil and fry for around 10 minutes or until golden brown and crispy. (If you're unsure, use a temperature probe to ensure the wings have reached an internal temperature of over 75°C/167°F.)

- Arrange the cooked wings on a wire rack over a baking tray and set aside in a low oven (150°C/Gas 2) to keep warm whilst you fry the second batch of wings.

- When all of the crispy wings are cooked, arrange in a serving basket, sprinkle with a little sea salt and serve. Alternatively, place the crispy wings in a bowl with your favourite wing sauce and toss to coat.

NASHVILLE HOT CHICKEN

Serves 1–2

Serving this chicken with just slices of bread might seem boring at first, but when the chicken packs this much of a kick, a simple bread slice and a few dill pickle slices becomes the perfect accompaniment!

100g plain flour
¼ teaspoon garlic powder
¼ teaspoon onion powder
¼ teaspoon dried Italian herbs (optional)
¼ teaspoon sea salt
¼ teaspoon black pepper
1 egg
3 tablespoons milk
1 teaspoon Frank's Red Hot Sauce
1 skinless, boneless chicken breast fillet (125g)
Vegetable oil for deep-frying
White or wholewheat bread and dill pickle slices, to serve

Cayenne Oil
2 teaspoons cayenne pepper
Pinch of smoked paprika
Pinch of paprika
Pinch of chilli powder
Pinch of garlic powder

Pinch of onion powder
1 tablespoon dark brown sugar

- First, prepare the spices for the cayenne oil. To a heatproof bowl, add the cayenne pepper, smoked paprika, paprika, chilli powder, garlic powder, onion powder and dark brown sugar. Mix well and set aside.

- For the chicken, place the plain flour, garlic powder, onion powder, Italian herbs (if desired), sea salt and black pepper in a large bowl. Mix well and transfer to a large plate.

- Add the egg, milk and hot sauce to a large bowl; mix well.

- With kitchen scissors, cut the chicken breast into 5–6 long strips. Keeping one hand dry and working one strip at a time, dip each strip in egg, then into the seasoned flour. Dip back in the egg once more and finally, into the seasoned flour to form a double breading. Repeat this process with each chicken strip and arrange the breaded strips on a plate. At this stage the chicken strips can be covered and set aside for several hours in the refrigerator before frying, if desired.

- Heat the oil for deep-frying to 180°C/350°F. Carefully place each chicken strip in the hot oil and fry for 4–5 minutes, turning occasionally, until golden brown and crispy. (If you're unsure, use a temperature probe and ensure the chicken has reached an internal temperature of over 75°C/167°F.) Remove the chicken strips from the pan, drain off any excess oil on kitchen paper and place on a heatproof plate.

- Allow the oil you used to fry the chicken to cool for 2–3 minutes whilst the chicken strips rest. Carefully spoon 4–5 tablespoons of the hot oil into the prepared cayenne spices and mix well. Immediately brush the cayenne oil generously onto the crispy chicken.

- Serve the hot chicken with bread and dill pickle slices.

BABY-BACK RIBS

Serves 2–4

2 small onions, peeled and quartered
6 garlic cloves, peeled and crushed
2 celery stalks, roughly chopped
1 apple, cored and roughly chopped (optional)
3 tablespoons sea salt
1½ teaspoons black pepper
1.5kg baby-back pork ribs
Good-quality BBQ sauce to finish (or make your own, page 215)
Coleslaw (page 106), to serve

- To a large stockpot, add the onions, garlic, celery, apple (no need to peel), sea salt and black pepper. Add the pork ribs to the pot and then add enough water to just cover them. Bring to a boil over a high heat, reduce to medium, cover and simmer for 1 hour.

- Preheat the oven to 150°C/Gas 2. Remove the ribs from the pot and arrange in a roasting dish; coat generously with BBQ sauce until almost completely covered. Cover the dish with foil and bake for 1 hour.

- Add a little more BBQ sauce and bake for a further 20–30 minutes, removing the foil for the last 10 minutes of cooking time, if desired. This allows the sauce to cook into the ribs and proves a more 'dry rib' finish. For saucy ribs, leave the foil on.

- Arrange the ribs on a large platter and serve with Coleslaw.

FRENCH FRIES

Serves 2

2 large floury potatoes (Maris Piper or King Edward are
   both good)
Vegetable oil for deep-frying
Sea salt, to serve

- First, peel the potatoes, slice and cut into thin sticks. Transfer to a bowl, rinse and cover with cold water. Set aside to soak for 2 hours, or cover and refrigerate overnight.

- Drain, pat dry with kitchen paper and set aside. Heat the oil for deep-frying to 150°C/300°F. When hot, carefully add the fries to the pan and fry for around 3–4 minutes or until just soft.

- Remove the fries from the pan, drain off any excess oil and set aside on a plate lined with kitchen paper. At this stage the fries can be cooled and stored in the refrigerator until needed (up to 2 days).

- To finish, heat the oil to 190°C/375°F. Carefully add the fries to the pan and fry for a further 2–3 minutes, or until golden and crispy. Remove the cooked fries from the pan, drain off any excess oil and tip on to a serving plate. Season generously with sea salt and serve.

Variations:

- Disco Fries – Top with Brown Gravy (page 234) and grated mozzarella cheese.
- Chilli-cheese Fries – Top with Chilli (page 195) and grated mozzarella cheese.

POTATO CHIPS

Serves 2

2 large floury potatoes (Maris Piper or King Edward are
   both good)
Vegetable oil for deep-frying
Sea salt, to serve

- Peel the potatoes and slice as thinly as possible (a mandolin
  will make this easier). Place the potato slices in a large
  bowl, cover with cold water and soak for 5 minutes. Drain
  and rinse, arrange on kitchen paper and pat dry.

- Heat the oil for deep-frying to 180°C/350°F. Working in
  small batches, carefully place the sliced potatoes in the hot
  oil and fry for 3–4 minutes, turning occasionally until crisp
  and golden. Remove the cooked chips from the pan, drain
  off any excess oil and transfer to kitchen paper.

- Whilst hot, season generously with sea salt and allow to
  cool slightly before serving with your favourite sandwich.

SWEET POTATO FRIES

Serves 2

2 large sweet potatoes
Vegetable oil for deep-frying
Sea salt and black pepper, to serve

- Peel the potatoes, slice and cut into thin sticks. Place in a bowl, rinse and cover with cold water. Set aside to soak for 1 hour.

- Drain the water, pat dry with kitchen paper and set aside. Heat the oil for deep-frying to 180°C/350°F. When hot, carefully add the fries to the pan and fry for around 3–4 minutes or until just soft.

- Remove the fries from the pan, drain off any excess oil and set aside on a plate lined with kitchen paper. At this stage the fries can be cooled and stored in the refrigerator until needed (up to 2 days).

- To finish, heat the oil to 190°C/375°F. Carefully add the fries to the pan and fry for a further 2–3 minutes, or until golden and crispy. Remove the cooked fries from the pan, drain off any excess oil and tip on to a serving plate. Season generously with sea salt and black pepper and serve.

MASHED POTATOES

Serves 2

Boiling the potatoes whole helps to ensure the mix is as dry as possible, which makes for a fluffier, lighter mash. American diners often use a product called 'half 'n' half' for their potatoes – you can replicate this at home by using a combination of milk and cream.

Any leftover mash will keep well for 2 days, or can be frozen. Simply reheat in a saucepan until piping hot, adding a little extra milk or cream as necessary, to achieve the desired consistency.

2 large floury potatoes (Maris Piper or King Edward are both good)
2 tablespoons salted butter, plus extra to serve
¼ teaspoon sea salt, plus extra for seasoning
Pinch of white pepper
300ml milk, plus extra as necessary
50ml single cream
Fresh chives, finely chopped, to garnish (optional)

- Fill a large saucepan with water. Add the potatoes, cover with water and season generously with sea salt.

- Cover the pan and bring it to a boil over a high heat. Reduce the heat to medium and boil the potatoes for 30–40 minutes or until tender. Drain and set aside to cool slightly before peeling.

- Return the peeled potatoes to the pan. Add the butter, sea salt and white pepper. Mash well, then add the milk and cream. Mix until the mash is smooth and no lumps remain, but avoid overworking or it will become gluey. Add more milk, if desired, for a thinner mash.

- Arrange the mashed potatoes on a serving plate. Use a teaspoon to press down lightly in the middle of the mash. Add a little extra piece of butter, garnish with chopped chives and serve.

TWICE-BAKED POTATOES

Serves 2

Crispy potato boats stuffed with bacon, cheese and spring onions.

2 baking potatoes
1 tablespoon vegetable oil
1 teaspoon sea salt, plus extra to season
60g Cheddar cheese, grated, plus extra to serve
60g mozzarella cheese, grated, plus extra to serve
4 tablespoons sour cream, plus extra to serve
2 spring onions, trimmed, peeled and finely sliced
Pinch of white pepper
Pinch of paprika

- Preheat the oven to 200°C/Gas 6. Rinse and pat dry the baking potatoes on kitchen paper. Rub with vegetable oil and sea salt and arrange directly on the middle rack of the oven with a baking tray underneath. Bake for around 1 hour to 1 hour 15 minutes, or until soft on the inside and crispy on the outside.

- Remove the potatoes from the oven and allow to cool slightly. Arrange on a baking tray and slice almost in half. Use a spoon to scoop out the cooked potato flesh, leaving a thin layer behind attached to the skin.

- Place the scooped potato flesh in a bowl. Add the Cheddar cheese, mozzarella cheese, sour cream and sliced spring onions. Season with a little extra salt, white pepper and paprika; mix well. Scoop the mixture back into the potato skins. At this stage the potatoes may be cooled completely and set aside in the refrigerator overnight for finishing the next day, if desired.

- Top the potato skins with a little extra cheese and place in a hot oven (200°C/Gas 6) for 10–12 minutes, or until the cheese has melted and the potato filling is piping hot. Serve the stuffed potato skins with a little extra sour cream on the side.

PAN-STEAMED BROCCOLI

Serves 1

Slightly smoky and charred, tender but with a little crunch remaining, this is a quick and easy method to cook your vegetable sides in just a few minutes. You could, of course, add some chopped garlic towards the end of the frying stage, if desired.

    Large handful broccoli florets (cut into small pieces)
    1 teaspoon olive oil
    1–2 tablespoons water
    Pinch of sea salt
    Pinch of black pepper
    Dash of lemon juice

- Rinse and pat dry the broccoli florets on kitchen paper. Heat the oil in a large deep frying pan over a medium heat. When hot, add the broccoli and cook for around 5 minutes.

- Add the water and cover the pan with a lid. Continue to cook the broccoli for a further 2–3 minutes, or until just tender. Season with salt and pepper and finish with a dash of lemon juice.

BBQ BEANS

Serves 4

Serve the BBQ Beans with steak (page 188) or Nashville Hot Chicken (page 73).

60g pancetta, diced
1 small onion, peeled and finely diced
400g tinned baked beans in tomato sauce
1 teaspoon yellow (American) mustard
1 tablespoon maple syrup
1 teaspoon soft brown sugar
1 tablespoon Worcestershire sauce
1 tablespoon apple cider vinegar
½ teaspoon paprika
½ teaspoon smoked paprika
¼ teaspoon garlic powder
Pinch of sea salt
Pinch of black pepper

- Set a frying pan over a medium heat to warm. Add the diced pancetta and onion. Stir-fry for 3–4 minutes.

- Add the remaining ingredients. Mix well and simmer for 5–6 minutes, or until well combined.

CHICKEN QUESADILLAS

Serves 2–4

1 skinless, boneless chicken breast fillet (125g)
1 teaspoon olive oil, plus extra for frying
1 small onion, peeled and sliced
½ red pepper, deseeded and sliced
½ green pepper, deseeded and sliced
1 teaspoon Cajun Seasoning (page 228)
1–2 tablespoons Sweet BBQ Sauce (page 215, optional)
4 large readymade flour tortillas
2 large handfuls grated mozzarella cheese
Sour cream, to serve

- First, slice the chicken into small pieces. Heat the oil in a large frying pan set over a medium heat. Add the chicken, onion, red and green peppers. Stir-fry for 3–4 minutes, or until the chicken is cooked and the vegetables are softened.

- Add the Cajun Seasoning, mix well and cook for a further minute, adding a little water, if necessary, if the pan gets too dry. Transfer the cooked chicken and vegetables to a plate and set aside to cool briefly. Add the Sweet BBQ Sauce, if desired.

- Heat a lightly greased frying pan over a medium heat. Place one flour tortilla in the pan. Spread half of the chicken and vegetable mix across the tortilla, top with a handful of grated mozzarella cheese and cover with another flour tortilla. Press down gently with a spatula and continue cooking the quesadilla for 2–3 minutes.

- Flip the quesadilla and continue to cook for a further 1–2 minutes on the other side, until the tortilla is crispy, the filling is hot and the cheese has melted.

- Cook the second quesadilla in the same way, cut each one into 4 quarters and serve with sour cream.

PIZZA QUESADILLA

Serves 1–2

2 readymade corn and wheat tortillas
1 teaspoon tomato ketchup (readymade or page xx)
1 teaspoon Sweet BBQ Sauce (page 215)
Small handful Cheddar cheese, grated
Small handful Gruyère cheese, grated
4 pepperoni slices
Pinch of black pepper
Pinch of dried oregano
1 teaspoon vegetable oil for frying

- Top one tortilla with ketchup and Sweet BBQ Sauce (mix and spread over the tortilla). Add half the Cheddar and Gruyère cheeses. Top with the pepperoni slices, then add the remaining cheese and season with black pepper and oregano. Top with the remaining tortilla.

- Heat a heavy griddle pan over a medium heat. When the pan is hot, brush with vegetable oil. Add the prepared quesadilla to the pan and toast for 2–3 minutes on each side, or until the quesadilla is crispy and charred and the cheese has melted.

- Set the quesadilla aside to rest for 2–3 minutes before slicing into quarters and serving.

3

SOUPS & SALADS

Whilst indulgent dishes such as pulled pork, fried chicken and cheeseburgers are ever tempting, there are occasions when something a little lighter is required. With the addition of delicious salad dressings, a diner salad becomes a thing of beauty indeed.

Matzo Ball Soup, also known as 'Jewish penicillin', is everything you already love about chicken soup, plus a whole lot more. With the addition of matzo balls and simple cracker bread-based dumplings, a bowl of soup becomes a hearty meal. Country Vegetable Soup provides a variety of nourishing vegetables and, of course, no soup menu would be complete without the classic Tomato Soup. Served with a simple grilled cheese sandwich (page 139), it's comfort food that's hard to beat!

COUNTRY VEGETABLE SOUP

Serves 6

This soup freezes well and can be heated thoroughly from frozen for a quick lunch.

6 large carrots, trimmed, peeled and diced
2 celery stalks, trimmed and diced
1 medium potato, peeled and diced
2 spring onions, trimmed, peeled and sliced
8 tablespoons red lentils
1.5 litres vegetable stock
Pinch of paprika
Pinch of dried parsley
Pinch of black pepper
1 litre of water
Dinner Rolls (page 238), to serve

- Place the carrots, celery, potato, spring onions, red lentils and vegetable stock in a large pot. Bring to the boil over a high heat and skim off any foam with a spoon.

- When the soup is boiling, reduce the heat to low, add the paprika, dried parsley and black pepper and mix well. Simmer for 1 hour.

- Mash well for a chunky soup, or allow to cool slightly before blending until completely smooth. Return the soup to the pot, add the water and simmer for a further 45 minutes or so, adding a little extra water, if necessary, until it reaches your desired consistency. Any leftover soup will thicken a little more in the refrigerator.

- Ladle the soup into serving bowls and serve with Dinner Rolls.

FRENCH ONION SOUP

Serves 2

1½ tablespoons salted butter
1 teaspoon olive oil
2 large Spanish onions, peeled and thinly sliced
Pinch of caster sugar
2 garlic cloves, peeled and crushed
1 tablespoon plain flour
125ml white wine
700ml beef stock
Pinch of dried thyme
Pinch of dried parsley
Pinch of black pepper
Dash of Worcestershire sauce
2–4 slices Country Bread (page 236)
2–4 slices of mozzarella or Gruyère cheese

- Heat the butter and olive oil in a large saucepan set over a medium heat. Add the sliced onions and sugar and cook for 30–40 minutes, stirring occasionally, until the onions are golden and caramelised. Add the crushed garlic and cook for a further minute.

- Add the plain flour and mix well to form a roux or thick paste. Cook for 2–3 minutes, stirring constantly. Add the white wine, beef stock, thyme, parsley, black pepper and

Worcestershire sauce. Bring to the boil, reduce the heat to low and simmer for 20–25 minutes.

- As the soup simmers, heat the grill on high. Toast the bread slices on one side. Ladle the soup into individual heatproof serving bowls and place the bread on top, toasted side down. Top generously with mozzarella or Gruyère and return to the grill for 2–3 minutes, or until the cheese is golden and has melted.

MATZO BALL SOUP

Serves 2

Matzo balls (simple cracker bread dumplings) are often easier to find in supermarkets than matzo meal. If this is the case, simply crush the crackers to a fine powder in a blender. If you've prepared your own chicken stock, spoon the fat from the top of the stock and use it for the matzo balls.

1 small onion, finely diced
1 large carrot, finely diced
1 celery stalk, finely diced
700ml chicken stock (from a cube or page 229)
Pinch of dried parsley
Pinch of black pepper
1 skinless, boneless chicken breast fillet (125g)

Matzo Balls
60g matzo meal (or 3 matzo crackers, blended into fine crumbs)
2 eggs
2 tablespoons chicken fat or vegetable oil
2 tablespoons chicken stock (from a cube or page 229)
Up to ¼ teaspoon baking powder (see Notes°)
Pinch of sea salt
Pinch of white pepper

- First, prepare the matzo balls. In a large bowl, combine matzo meal or ground matzo crackers, eggs, chicken fat or vegetable oil, chicken stock, baking powder, sea salt and white pepper. Use a fork to mix until well combined. Set the mix aside, uncovered, in the refrigerator for 1 hour.

- Place the diced onion, carrot and celery in a large pot. Add the chicken stock, dried parsley and black pepper, then the chicken breast fillet. Bring to the boil over a high heat, reduce the heat to low and simmer for 10–12 minutes.

- Remove the chicken breast from the soup and place on a chopping board. Shred the chicken on a plate with a knife and fork and return it to the soup.

- Using wet hands, scoop up tablespoon-sized amounts of the prepared matzo mix, roll into balls and drop carefully into the simmering soup. The prepared mixture should be enough to make 6 matzo balls. Cover the pot with a lid and simmer for around 30 minutes.

- Ladle the soup and matzo balls into serving bowls and serve immediately.

Notes

For dense matzo balls, leave out the baking powder. If you prefer very light matzo balls (known as 'floaters'), add ¼ teaspoon baking powder. For everything in between, add an amount between 0 and ¼ teaspoon!

CREAMY CHICKEN ORZO SOUP

Serves 4

Orzo is a short cut pasta, very popular in Greece. Its shape almost resembles large grains of rice and it works very well in soups or cold pasta salads.

- 2 sticks celery, trimmed and diced
- 2 carrots, trimmed and diced
- 1 small onion, peeled and finely diced
- 1 litre chicken stock (from a cube or page 229)
- ¼ teaspoon black pepper
- ½ teaspoon dried Italian herbs
- 2 skinless, boneless chicken breast fillets (each 125g)
- 100g dried orzo pasta
- 1 tablespoon fresh lemon juice
- 250ml milk (reserve 2 tablespoons)
- 1 teaspoon potato flour or cornflour

- Combine the diced celery, carrots, onion, chicken stock, black pepper and Italian herbs in a large pot. Mix well, bring to the boil over a high heat, then reduce to low. Add the chicken breast fillets and simmer for 12 minutes.

- Remove the chicken from the simmering stock and shred on a plate with a knife and fork into bite-sized pieces. Return the chicken to the stock. Add the orzo pasta and lemon juice and simmer for 3–4 minutes.

- Add the milk and mix well. Mix the reserved 2 tablespoons milk with 1 teaspoon potato flour or cornflour and add to the stock. Stir well and simmer for a further 5–6 minutes. Adjust the seasoning, if desired, and ladle the soup into serving bowls.

CORN CHOWDER

Serves 2

Chowder-style soup is typically made with cream and/or milk and is thickened almost like a gravy, resulting in a deliciously comforting broth.

   1 teaspoon vegetable oil
   4 slices smoked or unsmoked streaky bacon, diced
   1 small onion, peeled and finely diced
   1 stalk celery, trimmed and finely diced
   1 medium to large potato, peeled and finely diced
   ¼ teaspoon dried thyme
   ¼ teaspoon sea salt
   ¼ teaspoon black pepper
   1 tablespoon plain flour
   400ml chicken stock (from a cube or page 229)
   1 bay leaf
   175g sweetcorn kernels, fresh, tinned or frozen
   150ml milk
   1–2 tablespoons grated Parmesan cheese
   Dinner Rolls (page 238), to serve

- In a large pot, heat the vegetable oil over a low to medium heat. Add the diced bacon and stir-fry for 2–3 minutes. Add the diced onion and celery and stir-fry for a further 2–3 minutes. Add the diced potato, dried thyme, sea salt and black pepper and mix through.

- Add the plain flour and mix well. Simmer for 1–2 minutes until the flour gives off a slightly toasted aroma.

- Add the chicken stock, bay leaf and sweetcorn. Increase the heat briefly until the mixture comes to a boil, reduce the heat to low and simmer for 10–12 minutes.

- Remove the bay leaf. Add the milk and Parmesan cheese and simmer the chowder for 5–6 minutes until slightly thickened and creamy. Check the seasoning, ladle the soup into bowls and serve with Dinner Rolls.

SPLIT PEA SOUP

Serves 6–8

1 teaspoon salted butter
1 onion, peeled and finely chopped
2 large carrots, trimmed and sliced
2 celery stalks, trimmed and sliced
1 leek, trimmed and sliced
4 rashers smoked streaky bacon, chopped
2 garlic cloves, peeled and crushed
500g dried green split peas
2 litres chicken stock (from a cube or page 229)
2 bay leaves
½ teaspoon turmeric
1 teaspoon coriander powder
1 teaspoon dried Italian herbs
Pinch of sea salt
Pinch of black pepper
Lemon juice, to finish
Dinner Rolls (page 238), to serve

- Heat the butter in a large pot set over a medium heat. Add the onion, carrots, celery, leek and bacon. Cook for 5–6 minutes until the onions have softened and the bacon is well browned. Add the garlic and cook for a further minute.

- Add the split peas, chicken stock, bay leaves, turmeric, coriander, Italian herbs, sea salt and black pepper. Bring to the boil over a high heat, reduce the heat to low, cover and simmer the soup for around 1½ to 2 hours, stirring occasionally and adding a little water, if necessary.

- Just before serving, finish the soup off with a little lemon juice to lighten it up nicely. Check the seasoning, ladle into bowls and serve with Dinner Rolls.

TOMATO SOUP

Serves 4

750g cherry tomatoes, halved
4 garlic cloves, peeled and roughly chopped
1 onion, peeled and sliced
1 carrot, peeled and sliced
Pinch of dried Italian herbs
Pinch of sea salt
Pinch of black pepper
2 tablespoons olive oil
750ml chicken stock (from a cube or page 229)
1 bay leaf
Small handful fresh basil leaves, plus extra to garnish
Pinch of celery seed
1 teaspoon balsamic vinegar
Grilled Cheese Sandwiches (page 139), to serve

- Preheat the oven to 200°C/Gas 6. Arrange the cherry tomato halves on a roasting tray, cut sides facing upwards. Scatter the garlic, sliced onion and sliced carrots over the top of the tomatoes. Top with Italian herbs, sea salt and black pepper. Drizzle with olive oil, place the tray in the centre of the oven and roast for 20 minutes.

- Transfer the contents of the tray to a large pot. Add the chicken stock, bay leaf, fresh basil, celery seed and balsamic vinegar. Bring to the boil, reduce the heat to low and then simmer for 15–20 minutes.

- Blend the soup using a hand blender until completely smooth. Simmer for a further 5 minutes, ladle into serving bowls and garnish with a little extra fresh basil. Serve with Grilled Cheese Sandwiches on the side.

COLESLAW

Serves 2

The perfect accompaniment to Baby-back Ribs (page 76) or any good sandwich!

½ small onion, peeled and finely chopped
½ head white cabbage (roughly 400g), trimmed and finely
    shredded
2 large carrots, trimmed and grated
6 tablespoons mayonnaise
Dash of regular white (distilled) vinegar
Pinch of caster sugar
Pinch of sea salt
Pinch of white pepper

- Place all the ingredients in a large bowl. Mix thoroughly.

- Cover and set aside in the refrigerator for at least 1 hour before serving. After chilling, mix thoroughly once more and serve.

POTATO SALAD

Serves 2

Unlike British-style potato salad, typically made with baby new potatoes, American diner potato salad is often made with larger, floury Russet potatoes.

2 large floury potatoes (Maris Piper or King Edward are
   both good)
½ carrot, trimmed and grated
½ celery stick, trimmed and finely sliced
4 tablespoons mayonnaise
1 tablespoon Mustard Relish (page 223)
Pinch of caster sugar
Pinch of dried parsley
Pinch of sea salt, plus extra for seasoning
Pinch of black pepper
Dash of lemon juice
Pinch of paprika

- Fill a large pot with water. Add the potatoes, cover with water and season generously with sea salt.

- Cover the pot and bring to a boil over a high heat. Reduce the heat to medium and boil the potatoes for 30–40 minutes or until tender. Drain and set aside to cool slightly before peeling. Once peeled, chop into rough cubes.

- Place the grated carrot, sliced celery, mayonnaise, Mustard Relish, caster sugar, dried parsley, salt and black pepper in a large bowl. Mix well. Add the diced potatoes whilst still slightly warm and mix once more.

- Arrange the potato salad in a serving bowl, finish with lemon juice and paprika and then serve.

GARDEN SALAD

Serves 1

This is a good base salad, which would work well with the addition of hard-boiled eggs, grated Cheddar cheese or grilled meats.

1 Romaine lettuce, trimmed and shredded
5–6 cherry tomatoes, halved
½ cucumber, peeled and cubed
½ small red onion, peeled and finely sliced
1 small carrot, trimmed and sliced or grated
1 tablespoon Ranch Dressing (page 217)

- Place the lettuce, cherry tomatoes, cucumber, red onion and carrot in a large bowl. Mix well.

- Dress the salad with the Ranch Dressing and serve.

CAESAR SALAD

Serves 1

1 anchovy fillet, finely chopped
3 tablespoons mayonnaise
1 tablespoon grated Parmesan cheese, plus extra to
   garnish
Dash of Worcestershire sauce
¼ teaspoon Dijon mustard
1 teaspoon lemon juice
Pinch of sea salt
Pinch of black pepper
1 tablespoon olive oil
2 garlic cloves, peeled and crushed
2 slices white or wholewheat bread, cut into croutons
1 Romaine lettuce, shredded

- For the dressing, place the chopped anchovy, mayonnaise, Parmesan cheese, Worcestershire sauce, Dijon mustard, lemon juice, salt and black pepper in a large bowl. Mix well and set aside.

- Heat the oil in a frying pan set over a medium heat. Add the crushed garlic and fry for 1–2 minutes. Remove from the pan and set aside. Add the croutons to the pan and fry for 1–2 minutes, or until golden and toasted.

- Arrange the shredded Romaine lettuce on a serving plate. Add the prepared dressing and mix lightly. Top with toasted croutons. Finish with a little extra Parmesan cheese and serve.

COBB SALAD

Serves 1

1 skinless, boneless chicken breast fillet (125g)
1 teaspoon olive oil
1 teaspoon lemon juice
Pinch of sea salt
Pinch of black pepper
1 egg
Handful shredded iceberg lettuce
3 slices streaky bacon, cooked and diced (page 39)
1 salad tomato, deseeded and chopped
30g Roquefort cheese, crumbled
½ small avocado, pitted, peeled and sliced
1 spring onion, trimmed and finely sliced
1 tablespoon Ranch Dressing (page 217)

- Preheat the oven to 220°C/Gas 7. Place the chicken fillet on a baking tray and add the olive oil, lemon juice, sea salt and black pepper. Mix well until the chicken is evenly coated. Bake in the centre of the oven for 15–20 minutes or until cooked through, then set aside to cool. Once fully cooled, dice the chicken.

- Place the egg in a saucepan and cover with water. Bring to the boil, reduce the heat to low and simmer for 5–6 minutes. Drain, pour cold water over the egg and carefully peel. Set aside to cool. Once fully cooled, slice the egg.

- Arrange the iceberg lettuce on a serving plate. In rows, add the cooked bacon, cooked chicken, sliced egg, chopped tomato, crumbled blue cheese, sliced avocado and sliced spring onion. Dress the salad with Ranch Dressing and serve.

MACARONI SALAD

Serves 1

80g macaroni pasta (dry weight)
3 tablespoons mayonnaise
1½ teaspoons yellow (American) mustard
1½ teaspoons apple cider vinegar
Pinch of sea salt, plus extra to season
Pinch of black pepper
½ small onion, peeled and finely chopped
1 celery stalk, trimmed and finely sliced
½ carrot, peeled and finely chopped
¼ green pepper, deseeded and finely chopped
1–2 slices roasted red peppers from a jar, finely chopped

- Bring a large saucepan of water to the boil and season generously with sea salt. Add the macaroni pasta, stir once, reduce the heat to medium and boil according to the packet instructions until tender to the bite (al dente). Drain, rinse with cold water, drain again and set aside.

- To make the dressing, add the mayonnaise, yellow (American) mustard, apple cider vinegar, sea salt and black pepper to a bowl. Mix well.

- Place the cooked pasta and dressing in a large dish; mix well. Add the chopped onion, sliced celery, chopped carrot, green pepper and roasted red pepper. Mix well once more, cover and set aside in the refrigerator for at least 1 hour or, preferably, overnight.

• Remove the macaroni pasta from the refrigerator 30 minutes before serving to get up to room temperature.

4

BURGERS, HOT DOGS & SANDWICHES

The diner method of cooking burger patties on a flat-top grill can be easily replicated at home using a heavy frying pan. I've experimented with various burger recipes and enjoyed many of them, but it's hard to beat a properly smashed diner-style burger. The sear on the meat ensures that the burger remains juicy during cooking, adding a smoky flavour to the finished burger at the same time. If you're serious about making a quality burger or hot dog, making your own buns or rolls is highly recommended (page 240).

Diner sandwiches are a thing of beauty, packed high with meats and served with enough potato chips and pickles to turn a snack into an entire meal. Of course, as with all simple recipes, the quality of the ingredients matters, so be sure to find the best deli-style meats you can.

SLIDERS

Serves 1 (Makes 3 sliders)

These mini cheeseburgers are as cute as they are delicious. Slider buns aren't widely available in the UK, but a good-quality hot dog bun, sliced into three small slider rolls, is an ideal substitute. Alternatively, make your own slider buns (page 240) and divide the dough into 16 smaller buns. A single slice of cheese is enough for 3 buns.

113g beef mince (20 per cent fat)
1 teaspoon vegetable oil
¼ teaspoon sea salt
¼ teaspoon black pepper
1 onion, peeled and very thinly sliced
1 slice cheese (Monterey Jack or processed), divided into 3
1 hot dog bun, cut into three equal pieces or 3 homemade
    slider sized Burger Buns (page 240)
Handful gherkin slices (dill pickles), tomato ketchup
    (readymade or page 210) and French Fries (page 78),
    to serve

- Divide the beef mince into three portions. With your hands, form each one into a meatball.

- Heat a large, heavy frying pan over a high heat until just beginning to smoke. Add the vegetable oil, reduce the heat to medium and add the prepared meatballs to the pan. Carefully smash each meatball down into a thin patty using a spatula (I wrap greaseproof paper around my spatula to help prevent sticking). Once smashed, season generously with sea salt and black pepper and top with the thinly sliced onions. Fry the patties for 2–3 minutes.

- Unwrap the greaseproof paper from your spatula. Scrape and flip each onion-topped burger patty. Top each one with a piece of cheese, cover the pan with a lid and continue to cook for a further 2 minutes.

- Remove the lid from the pan and top each burger patty with the bottom half of your sliced rolls. Place the remaining bun halves on top to warm slightly. After about a minute, use your spatula to scrape the onion and burger patties and immediately flip into the bread rolls.

- Serve the sliders with a handful of gherkin slices (dill pickles) tomato ketchup and French Fries.

SMASHED BURGER

Serves 1

This classic burger searing technique delivers perfect results every time!

1 teaspoon vegetable oil
113g beef mince (20 per cent fat)
¼ teaspoon sea salt, plus extra to season
¼ teaspoon black pepper
1 small onion, peeled and very thinly sliced
1 cheese slice (Monterey Jack or processed)
1 large sesame seed burger bun (make your own, page 240)
1 tablespoon Burger Sauce (page 220)
Handful shredded iceberg lettuce
2 tomato slices
Handful gherkin slices (dill pickles), tomato ketchup (readymade or page 210) and French Fries (page 78), to serve

- Using your hands, form the beef mince into a meatball.

- Heat a large, heavy frying pan over a high heat until just beginning to smoke. Add the vegetable oil, reduce the heat to medium and add the mince to the pan. Carefully smash the mince down into a thin patty using a spatula (I wrap greaseproof paper around my spatula to help prevent sticking). Once smashed, season with sea salt and black pepper and top with thinly sliced onion. Fry for 5 minutes.

- Unwrap the greaseproof paper from your spatula. Scrape and flip the onion-topped burger patty. Top the patty with the cheese slice, cover the pan with a lid and continue cooking for a further 3–4 minutes.

- Meanwhile, in a separate dry pan, toast the burger bun over a medium heat until the insides are golden and charred. Spread Burger Sauce over the bottom half of the bun and top with shredded lettuce and tomato slices.

- Place the undressed burger bun half on top of the burger. Use your spatula to scrape the onions and burger from the pan, place on top of the dressed burger bun half and serve.

- Serve the smashed burger with a handful of gherkin slices (dill pickles), tomato ketchup and French Fries.

NAKED CHICKEN BURGER

Serves 1

A light and healthy burger, still packed full of flavour, thanks to a slow marinate in a smoky-sweet sauce.

1 teaspoon vegetable oil
75ml water
3 tablespoons tomato ketchup (readymade or page 210)
¼ teaspoon dried Italian herbs
¼ teaspoon paprika
¼ teaspoon smoked paprika
Pinch of onion powder
Pinch of garlic powder
Pinch of sea salt
Pinch of black pepper
1 skinless, boneless chicken breast fillet (125g)
Vegetable oil for frying
1 sesame seed Burger Bun (page 240)
1 tablespoon Black Pepper Mayo (page 216)
Handful shredded iceberg lettuce
2–3 tomato slices
French Fries (page 78) and Coleslaw (page 106), to serve

- To make the marinade, place the vegetable oil, water, tomato ketchup, Italian herbs, paprika, smoked paprika, onion powder, garlic powder, sea salt and black pepper in a large bowl. Mix well and set aside.

- Place the chicken breast on a large piece of greaseproof paper. Cover with another layer of greaseproof paper and use a meat hammer or heavy rolling pin to pound the chicken flat, around 5mm thick. Add the chicken to the prepared marinade, cover and set aside in the refrigerator for at least 4 hours, or ideally, overnight.

- Heat a lightly greased, heavy griddle pan over a high heat. When piping hot, turn the heat down to medium. Carefully lift the chicken out of the marinade, allowing any excess to drain off. Carefully place the chicken on the hot griddle and cook for around 2–3 minutes on each side, or until cooked through (the juices will run clear when pierced with a fork) and slightly charred.

- In a separate dry pan, toast the burger bun over a medium heat until the insides are golden and charred. Spread Black Pepper Mayo over the bottom bun and top with shredded lettuce and tomato slices.

- Lift the chicken burger onto the dressed bun half, top with the remaining bun half and serve with French Fries and Coleslaw.

CRISPY CHICKEN BURGER

Serves 1

100g plain flour
¼ teaspoon garlic powder
¼ teaspoon onion powder
¼ teaspoon dried Italian herbs (optional)
Pinch of cayenne pepper
¼ teaspoon sea salt
¼ teaspoon black pepper
1 egg
3 tablespoons milk
1 teaspoon Frank's Red Hot Sauce
1 skinless, boneless chicken breast fillet (125g)
Vegetable oil for deep-frying
1 large sesame seed burger bun (or make your own, page 240)
1 tablespoon mayonnaise
Pinch of onion powder
Handful shredded iceberg lettuce
Coleslaw (page 106) and French Fries (page 78), to serve

- Place the plain flour, garlic powder, onion powder, Italian herbs (if desired), cayenne pepper, sea salt and black pepper in a large bowl. Mix well and transfer to a large plate.

- Place the egg, milk and hot sauce in a large bowl; mix well.

- Place the chicken breast on a large piece of greaseproof paper. Cover with another layer of greaseproof paper and use a meat hammer or heavy rolling pin to pound the chicken flat, around 5mm thick. Keeping one hand dry, dip the chicken in the egg and then in the seasoned flour. Dip the chicken back in the egg once more and finally, in the seasoned flour to form a double breading. At this stage the chicken burger can be covered and set aside for several hours in the refrigerator before frying, if desired.

- Heat the oil for deep-frying to 180°C/350°F. Carefully place the chicken burger in the hot oil and fry for 4–5 minutes, turning once, or until the chicken is cooked (the juices will run clear when pierced with a fork) and the breading is golden and crispy. Remove the crispy chicken burger from the pan and set aside on a wire rack to rest for 2 minutes.

- In a separate dry pan, toast the burger bun over a medium heat until the insides are golden and charred. Mix the mayonnaise and onion powder and spread over one burger bun half. Top with shredded lettuce.

- Place the burger on top of the dressed bun. Add the remaining bun half, flip and serve.

- Serve the crispy chicken burger with Coleslaw and French Fries.

Variation: Spicy Chicken Burger – Prepare a spiced oil as per Nashville Hot Chicken (page 73) and brush the fried chicken burger generously with it before assembling the burger.

VEGGIE BURGER PATTIES

Makes 2

A delicious vegetarian alternative to the Smashed Burger recipe (page 120). Serve a selection of both at your BBQ!

1 x 400g tin chickpeas
½ teaspoon garlic paste
½ teaspoon ground cumin
½ teaspoon ground coriander
Pinch of cayenne pepper
½ teaspoon sea salt
Pinch of black pepper
2–3 tablespoons gram (chickpea) flour, plus extra for
   shaping
Vegetable oil for deep-frying
2 large sesame seed burger buns (or make your own, page
   240)
2 tablespoons Burger Sauce (page 220)
2 handfuls iceberg lettuce
4 tomato slices
Handful gherkin slices (dill pickles), tomato ketchup
   (readymade or page 210) and French Fries (page 78),
   to serve

- Place the chickpeas, garlic paste, cumin, coriander, cayenne, sea salt and black pepper in a large bowl. Mash thoroughly with a potato masher until almost smooth. Add the gram (chickpea) flour and mix once more.

- Dust your hands with a little more gram (chickpea) flour and form 2 balls from the mix. Pat each ball down into a patty shape, arrange on a plate, cover and set aside in the refrigerator for 2 hours to firm up.

- Heat the oil to 180°C/350°F and deep-fry the veggie patties for 3–4 minutes until crispy and golden. Meanwhile, in a separate dry pan, toast the burger buns over a medium heat until the insides are golden and charred. Spread one half of each burger bun with Burger Sauce, top with shredded lettuce and tomato slices. Finally, place the cooked veggie burger patties on top.

- Place the 2 undressed burger bun halves on top of each filled burger. Serve with gherkin slices (dill pickles), tomato ketchup and French Fries.

CONEY ISLAND HOT DOGS

Serves 3

The beef sauce detailed below makes enough for 3 hot dogs. Any leftover sauce will keep well in a sealed container in the refrigerator for up to 2 days.

1 onion, peeled and chopped
250g beef mince
Pinch of cumin
Pinch of onion powder
Pinch of celery seed
¼ teaspoon sea salt
Pinch of black pepper
100ml tomato ketchup (readymade or page 210)
1 tablespoon yellow (American) mustard
1 teaspoon caster sugar
1 tablespoon apple cider vinegar
Dash of Worcestershire sauce
2 tablespoons water

To serve (per person)
1 good-quality jumbo hot dog
1 Hot Dog Roll (page 240)
1 tablespoon grated Cheddar cheese
1 tablespoon chopped onions
Tomato ketchup (readymade or page 210) or yellow
   (American) mustard (optional)

- To make the sauce, heat a large saucepan over a high heat. Add the chopped onion and beef mince. Fry for 2–3 minutes until the mince has browned. Drain off any excess fat.

- Add the cumin, onion powder, celery seed, sea salt, black pepper, tomato ketchup, yellow (American) mustard, caster sugar, apple cider vinegar, Worcestershire sauce and water. Mix well and bring to the boil. Once boiling, reduce the heat to low and simmer the sauce for around 45–50 minutes or until thickened.

To assemble a Coney Island Hot Dog:
- Bring a large saucepan of water to the boil and add 1 good-quality jumbo hot dog. Reduce the heat to medium and simmer the hot dog for around 7 minutes or until piping hot.

- Dampen a sliced hot dog roll with a few drops of water and wrap in kitchen paper. Microwave on full power for 20–30 seconds to soften. Alternatively, add a steamer pan above the simmering hot dog and steam the bun for 1 minute.

- Arrange the hot dog roll on a serving basket and add the hot dog. Top with the beef sauce, followed by a handful of grated Cheddar cheese. Finally, add the chopped raw onion, finish with ketchup or yellow (American) mustard, if desired, and serve.

JERSEY-STYLE RIPPER

Serves 1

Vegetable oil for deep-frying
1 good-quality jumbo hot dog
1 Hot Dog Roll (page 240)
1 processed cheese slice (optional)
2 tablespoons Mustard Relish (page 223)

- Heat the oil for deep-frying to 180°C/350°F. Pat the hot dog dry with kitchen paper and place carefully in the hot oil. Fry for 3–4 minutes or until dark all over – the dog may sometimes burst open slightly when it's ready, hence the term 'ripper'. It's a good idea to use a splash guard when deep-frying the hot dogs as they do tend to pop a little when fully cooked.

- Dampen a sliced hot dog roll with a few drops of water and wrap in kitchen paper. Microwave on full power for 20–30 seconds to soften the roll.

- Remove the cooked hot dog from the pan, drain off any excess oil and place inside the warmed hot dog roll. Add the cheese slice, if desired. Top with Mustard Relish and serve.

CHICAGO DOG

Serves 1

A Chicago dog isn't a Chicago dog without a poppyseed roll – luckily, you can ensure you have yours by making your own (page 240). If you can find gherkin slices (dill pickles), then it's traditional to add these to the dog too.

1 good-quality jumbo hot dog
1 large poppyseed-topped hot dog roll (page 240)
2 teaspoons yellow (American) mustard
4 gherkin slices (dill pickles), finely chopped
½ small onion, peeled and finely chopped
1 small salad tomato, quartered
3–4 pickled jalapeño slices (or 'sports peppers', if you can find them)
Pinch of celery salt
French Fries (page 78) or Potato Chips (page 80), to serve

- Bring a large saucepan of water to the boil and add the jumbo hot dog. Reduce the heat to medium and simmer for around 7 minutes, or until piping hot.

- Dampen a sliced poppyseed-topped hot dog roll with a few drops of water and wrap in kitchen paper. Microwave on full power for 20–30 seconds to soften the roll. Alternatively, add a steamer pan above the simmering hot dog and steam the bun for 1 minute.

- Arrange the hot dog roll on a serving basket and add the hot dog. Top with yellow (American) mustard, gherkin slices (dill pickles), chopped onion, tomatoes, pickled jalapeño slices and celery salt. Serve with French Fries or Potato Chips.

CHEESESTEAK

Serves 1

For a veggie cheese steak, replace the steak with sliced mushrooms.

1 sirloin steak (200–225g)
1 teaspoon vegetable oil
1 teaspoon salted butter
1 onion, peeled and finely sliced
½ green pepper, deseeded and diced (optional)
Pinch of sea salt
Pinch of black pepper
1–2 provolone (Italian cheese) or processed cheese slices
1 large French bread roll or Hot Dog Roll (page 240)
Potato Chips (page 80), to serve

- Place the sirloin steak in the freezer for around 1 hour or until just beginning to freeze. Remove from the freezer and slice as thinly as possible. Set aside.

- Heat the vegetable oil and butter in a heavy frying pan set over a medium heat. Add the sliced onion and chopped pepper, if desired. Stir-fry for 7–8 minutes, or until charred. Increase the heat to high, add the steak slices, season with sea salt and black pepper and stir-fry for 2–3 minutes or until the steak slices are just cooked through.

- Use a spatula to bring all the ingredients together in the pan, roughly shaped to the size of your roll. Top the mix with cheese slices. Split open the French bread or Hot Dog Roll and place it on top of the cheese-topped mix. Allow the heat from the pan to steam the roll for around 1 minute – as this happens, the cheese-topped filling will begin to glue itself to the bread roll, making assembly easier.

- After 1–2 minutes when the cheese has melted, use your spatula to quickly lift all of the ingredients into the roll, flipping the contents over as you do so. Serve with Potato Chips.

CHICKEN PHILLY

Serves 1

1 skinless, boneless chicken breast fillet (125g)
2 teaspoons vegetable oil
½ small onion, peeled and chopped
¼ green pepper, deseeded and chopped
¼ red pepper, deseeded and chopped
1 teaspoon Cajun Seasoning (page 228)
1–2 provolone (Italian cheese) or processed cheese slices
1 large French bread roll or Hot Dog Roll (page 240)
Potato Chips (page 80), to serve

- Cut the chicken breast into small bite-sized pieces. Heat the vegetable oil in a wok or large frying pan set over a medium to high heat. Add the chicken, chopped onion, green and red peppers. Stir-fry for 3–4 minutes, or until the chicken is cooked and the vegetables are charred. Reduce the heat to low, add the Cajun Seasoning and stir-fry for a further minute. Add 1 teaspoon of water if the mixture becomes too dry.

- Use a spatula to bring all the ingredients together in the pan, roughly shaped to the size of your roll. Top the mix with the cheese slices. Split open your French bread or hot dog roll and place it on top of the cheese-topped mix. Allow the heat from the pan to steam the roll for around 1 minute

– as this happens, the cheese-topped filling will begin to glue itself to the bread roll, making assembly easier.

- After 1–2 minutes when the cheese has melted, use your spatula to quickly lift all of the ingredients into the roll, flipping the contents over as you do so. Serve the Chicken Philly with Potato Chips.

BLT

Serves 1

A classic in every way, bacon, lettuce and tomato combines to create a sandwich which is more than the sum of its parts!

2 slices of your favourite bread (I like brown or whole-
    meal Polish-style bread)
1 tablespoon salted butter
1 tablespoon mayonnaise
Handful shredded iceberg lettuce
4 slices of tomato
Pinch of sea salt
Pinch of black pepper
3–4 slices smoked or unsmoked bacon (page 39)
Potato Chips (page 80) and pickles, to serve

- Toast the bread until golden on both sides. Allow to cool slightly before spreading 1 slice with salted butter and the other with mayonnaise.

- Arrange the shredded lettuce on one slice of bread. Top with sliced tomato and season with salt and pepper. Add the cooked bacon and top with the remaining bread slice.

- Slice the sandwich into two triangles and arrange on a serving plate. Serve with Potato Chips and pickles.

GRILLED CHEESE SANDWICH

Serves 1

Any combination of your favourite cheeses will make a nice sandwich, however the combination described below ensures flavour from the Cheddar and stretchy, meltiness from the Monterey Jack and mozzarella.

2 tablespoons mayonnaise
2 slices white or wholewheat bread
1–2 slices Cheddar cheese
1 slice Monterey Jack cheese
Small handful grated mozzarella cheese
Pinch of sea salt
Pinch of black pepper
Pinch of white pepper
Tomato Soup (page 104), to serve

- Heat a dry frying pan over a medium heat. Spread 1 tablespoon of mayonnaise over a slice of bread and place in the pan, mayonnaise side down. Top with Cheddar cheese, Monterey Jack cheese and grated mozzarella. Season with sea salt, black and white pepper. Spread the remaining tablespoon of mayonnaise over the other bread slice and place it on top to form a sandwich, mayonnaise side up.

- Let the grilled cheese sandwich cook for 3–4 minutes, turning once or until the cheese has melted and the bread is golden. For an extra-cheesy sandwich, top the sandwich with another slice of Cheddar, carefully flip the sandwich in the pan once more and allow the cheese to catch on the bottom of the pan. This slightly messy affair is optional but results in a beautiful crispy cheese layer to your grilled cheese.

- Arrange the sandwich on a serving plate and slice diagonally to form two triangles. Press down a little in the middle of each slice so that some of the melted cheese comes out. Push the sandwich slices back together (a trick diners often use in order to ensure a stretchy, stringy cheese effect when the sandwich is pulled apart by the customer).

- Serve the sandwich with Tomato Soup (page 104).

PATTY MELT (HAMBURGER-FILLED GRILLED CHEESE SANDWICH)

Serves 1

Tiny Naylor, a Los Angeles restaurateur, is widely considered to have invented, or at least popularised, this burger sandwich in the 1940s.

113g beef mince (20 per cent fat)
1 teaspoon vegetable oil
½ teaspoon sea salt
¼ teaspoon black pepper
½ small onion, peeled and very thinly sliced
1 teaspoon salted butter
2 slices white, wholewheat or rye bread
2 Swiss cheese slices

- First, shape the beef mince into a meatball. Heat a large, heavy frying pan over a high heat until just beginning to smoke. Add the vegetable oil, reduce the heat to medium and place the prepared meatball in the pan.

- Carefully smash the meatball down into a thin patty using a spatula (I wrap greaseproof paper around my spatula to help prevent sticking). Once smashed, season generously with sea salt and black pepper and top with the thinly sliced onion. Fry the patty for 4 minutes.

- Unwrap the greaseproof paper from your spatula. Scrape and flip the onion-topped burger patty. Cover the pan with a lid and cook the patty for a further 3 minutes. Remove from the pan and set aside.

- Now, add the salted butter to the pan the burger patty was cooked in. Add a bread slice to the pan. Top with a slice of cheese, then add the cooked patty; top with another slice of cheese and the remaining bread slice.

- Cook the patty melt in the pan for 2–3 minutes or until the bread is golden on the bottom. Carefully flip and cook for a further 1–2 minutes on the other side or until golden all over. Remove the patty melt from the pan, slice and serve.

TUNA MELT

Serves 2

160g tinned tuna in spring water, drained
½ small onion, peeled and finely chopped
½ celery stalk, trimmed and finely chopped
4 tablespoons mayonnaise
1 teaspoon yellow (American) mustard
Pinch of sea salt
Pinch of black pepper
4 slices white or wholewheat bread
4 slices Gouda cheese
1 salad tomato, sliced
Potato Chips (page 80), to serve

- To make the tuna salad, place the tuna, onion, celery, mayonnaise, yellow (American) mustard, sea salt and black pepper in a large bowl. Mix well.

- Preheat the grill to high. Toast the bread slices on one side until golden and crisp. Turn over and toast briefly for a few seconds. Remove from the grill and top each lightly grilled slice with the prepared tuna salad, then top with 1 slice cheese and sliced tomato.

- Place the bread under the grill once more for 2–3 minutes, or until the cheese has melted and the Tuna Melts are piping hot. Serve with Potato Chips on the side.

REUBEN SANDWICH

Serves 1

2 slices wholewheat or rye-style bread
1 tablespoon salted butter, plus extra for frying
1 tablespoon Thousand Island dressing
2 slices Swiss-style cheese
3 slices deli-style corned beef
1 tablespoon sauerkraut, drained
1 teaspoon vegetable oil
Pickle slices and Potato Chips (page 80), to serve

- Arrange the bread slices on a work surface. Spread 1 slice of bread with butter and spread Thousand Island dressing on the other. To the buttered bread, add 1 slice of Swiss cheese, all of the corned beef and sauerkraut and finally, the remaining slice of cheese to form a sandwich.

- Heat the oil and a touch more salted butter in a heavy frying pan set over a medium heat. Carefully place the sandwich in the pan and cook for 3–4 minutes, turning once or until the cheese has melted and the bread is golden.

- Arrange the sandwich on a serving plate and slice diagonally to form two triangles. Serve with pickle slices and Potato Chips.

Variation: Rachel Sandwich – Use pastrami instead of corned beef and Coleslaw (page 106) in place of sauerkraut.

HOT TURKEY SANDWICH

Serves 2

2 tablepoons salted butter (or leftover fat from cooked
    bacon, etc)
2 tablespoons plain flour
300–350ml chicken stock (from a cube or page 229)
Pinch of garlic powder
Pinch of dried Italian herbs
Pinch of black pepper
5–6 slices deli-style turkey breast
2 slices white or wholewheat bread

- Heat the butter or fat in a heavy frying pan set over a medium heat. Once melted, add the plain flour, whisking constantly. Cook the mixture for at least 3–4 minutes, whisking constantly, until the flour cooks out and a toasted and nutty aroma fills the air.

- Remove the pan from the heat and slowly add the chicken stock, whisking constantly. Return the pan to the heat, add the garlic powder, Italian herbs and black pepper and simmer for 2–3 minutes or until the gravy thickens, adding a little more stock as necessary, if it thickens too quickly.

- As the gravy simmers, hold one turkey slice at a time with a pair of tongs and warm slightly in the gravy. Place the bread slices on plates. Arrange the warmed turkey over the bread, cover generously with more gravy and serve.

MONTE CRISTO SANDWICH

Serves 1

This sweet and savoury sandwich is dipped in batter and French-toasted in its entirety! Yes, it sounds bizarre, but it's absolutely delicious!

2 slices brioche or white bread
1 tablespoon mayonnaise
1 tablespoon Dijon mustard
4 slices deli-style ham
2 slices Swiss-style cheese
1 egg
3 tablespoons milk
Pinch of cinnamon
Pinch of nutmeg
Pinch of caster sugar
¼ teaspoon sea salt
Pinch of black pepper
1 tablespoon vegetable oil
1 tablespoon salted butter
Icing sugar and fruit jam, to serve

- Spread 1 slice of brioche or bread with mayonnaise and the other with Dijon mustard. Add the ham and cheese and combine to make a basic sandwich.

- In a shallow dish, combine the egg, milk, cinnamon, nutmeg, caster sugar, sea salt and black pepper. Mix well.

- Heat the oil and butter in a heavy frying pan set over a medium heat. When hot, dip the entire sandwich in the prepared batter and carefully place in the pan. Fry for 2–3 minutes on each side or until the bread is golden and the cheese has melted.

- Slice the sandwich into two triangles and arrange on a serving plate. Dust with sifted icing sugar and serve with fruit jam on the side.

TAYLOR HAM, EGG & CHEESE

Serves 1

A New Jersey classic, this sandwich is also referred to as a 'Pork Roll, Egg & Cheese' depending on your locale. Taylor ham is a smoky pork product not available in the UK – Canadian bacon, Brunswick ham or a good smoked streaky bacon provide a nice substitute.

1 teaspoon vegetable oil
1 teaspoon salted butter
1 bread roll, sliced and toasted
1 egg
Pinch of sea salt
Pinch of black pepper
Pinch of white pepper
1 processed cheese slice
2 slices Canadian bacon, Brunswick ham or smoked streaky bacon, cooked (page 39)
Tomato ketchup (readymade or page 210, optional)

- Heat the vegetable oil and butter in a frying pan set over a medium heat. Once the butter has melted, place the sliced bread roll in the pan, insides facing down. Toast in the oil and butter for 1–2 minutes until golden and crispy. Remove and keep warm.

- Add a touch more oil if the pan is too dry and then crack the egg into the pan and season with salt, black pepper and white pepper. Cover with a lid and cook for 1 minute.

- Remove the lid from the pan and top the egg with the processed cheese. Top with Canadian bacon, Brunswick ham or smoked streaky bacon. Cover the pan with the lid once more and cook for a further minute, until the egg is just cooked and the cheese has melted.

- Use a spatula to scrape the ham, egg and cheese out of the frying pan and into the toasted roll. Serve with ketchup, if desired.

FRENCH DIP

Serves 1

When time is short, you could use shop-bought deli-style roast beef and a simple beef stock dip to make quick sandwiches. To do things right though, take the time to make the brisket yourself and don't lose a drop of the flavourful onion gravy it is cooked in!

1 bread roll, French bread-style
1 slice Swiss-style cheese (optional)
2 ladles brisket onion gravy (page 182) or beef stock
5–6 slices beef brisket (page 182) or deli-style roast beef
Spicy mustard or Mustard Relish (page 223) and pickle
    slices, to serve

- Slice the French bread roll in half and toast under a hot grill for 1–2 minutes until golden. Add the cheese slice, if desired, and grill for a further 30 seconds until the cheese has melted slightly. Set the toasted roll aside on a serving plate.

- Heat the brisket onion gravy or beef stock in a small saucepan, adding water as necessary to thin it out a little. Once the gravy is simmering, add the beef slices and simmer for 1–2 minutes, or until piping hot.

- With tongs, lift the beef slices out of the sauce and arrange on the French bread. Form a sandwich and serve with the onion gravy on the side for dipping. Alternatively, serve 'wet' by holding the sandwich with a pair of tongs and dipping the entire sandwich, bread and all, into the simmering onion gravy.

• Serve with spicy mustard or Mustard Relish and pickle slices.

PO' BOY

Serves 1

1 large French bread roll
1 tablespoon garlic butter (page 170)
4 tablespoons plain flour
4 tablespoons Panko breadcrumbs
1 teaspoon Cajun Seasoning (page 228), plus a little extra
    to serve
1 egg, mixed with 3 tablespoons milk
165g raw, peeled King prawns
Vegetable oil for deep-frying
1 tablespoon Remoulade (page 219)
Handful shredded iceberg lettuce
3–4 slices of tomato
Pickle slices, to serve

- Preheat the oven to 200°C/Gas 6. Split the bread roll in half and spread with garlic butter.

- Place the plain flour, Panko breadcrumbs and Cajun Seasoning in a bowl. Mix well and transfer to a large plate.

- Place the egg and milk mixture in a large bowl; mix well. Keeping one hand dry and working one at a time, dip the King prawns in the seasoned flour and breadcrumbs, then in the egg and then back in the seasoned flour and breadcrumbs.

- Heat the oil for deep-frying to 180°C/350°F. Carefully place the breaded prawns in the hot oil and fry for 2–3 minutes, turning occasionally until the prawns are cooked and the breading is golden and crispy.

- Meanwhile, bake the garlic buttered roll in the oven for 3–4 minutes. Spread the roll with Remoulade and then fill with shredded iceberg lettuce and tomato slices.

- Remove the prawns from the pan, drain off any excess oil and add to the roll. Dust with a little extra Cajun Seasoning and serve with pickle slices.

FRY BREAD TACOS

Serves 2

½ teaspoon cornflour
½ teaspoon garlic powder
½ teaspoon onion powder
½ teaspoon cumin
¼ teaspoon paprika
½ teaspoon smoked paprika
Pinch of dried oregano
Pinch of cayenne pepper
Pinch of chilli powder
Pinch of sea salt
Pinch of black pepper
250g beef mince
125ml beef stock
1 prepared Pizza Dough ball (page 159)
Flour for rolling out
Vegetable oil for frying
2 large handfuls shredded iceberg lettuce
1 salad tomato, diced
1 red onion, peeled and finely chopped
Sour cream, lime wedges and guacamole, to serve

- Place the cornflour, garlic powder, onion powder, cumin, paprika, smoked paprika, oregano, cayenne pepper, chilli powder, sea salt and black pepper in a large bowl. Mix well.

- Heat a large pot over a medium-high heat. Add the beef mince and fry for 2–3 minutes, or until well browned. Drain off any excess oil and return the pot to the heat. Add the prepared spice mix and cook for 1 minute, stirring constantly.

- Add the beef stock, bring the mixture to the boil and reduce the heat to low. Simmer for around 15 minutes, stirring occasionally. At this stage, the meat may be cooled and stored in the refrigerator for up to 2 days, or in the freezer for up to 1 month – reheat until piping hot when needed.

- Divide the pizza dough into 4 equal pieces. Fill a wok or frying pan one third full with oil and heat to around 180°C/350°F. On a floured surface, roll out the pizza dough pieces to thin 15cm rounds. Carefully place 1 piece of dough in the pan and immediately spoon hot oil over the top – the bread will puff up quickly. Fry for around 20–30 seconds, then carefully flip the bread over. Fry for a further 20–30 seconds, remove from the pan and set aside on kitchen paper. Repeat the process until all of the fry breads are cooked.

- To serve the fry bread tacos, arrange 2 fry breads on each serving plate. Top generously with the mince, followed by shredded lettuce, diced tomato and chopped red onion. Serve with all the fixings!

5

PIZZA & PASTA

A good pizza is, in general, a simple affair – crusty, chewy bread, sweet tomato sauce, stretchy, melting cheese and a selection of our own favoured toppings. Of course, the dough is all-important and this chapter includes recipes for both traditional pan and deep-dish pizzas.

When it comes to cooking pizza at home, the battle rages on: home ovens just don't get hot enough to cook a pizza like a proper wood-fired or commercial pizza oven. In truth, the temperature doesn't even get close. So, other means and measures must be explored. The best result, after much testing, is the pan pizza: by allowing the dough to prove for a final time in a greased frying pan or crepe pan, heat can be applied directly to the pan. As the oil in the pan gets hot, the dough begins to lightly fry and puff up, creating a perfectly golden and charred pizza crust. If you really want to ensure a well-fired crust, a cook's blowtorch applied briefly as soon as the pizza leaves the oven will do the job!

Deep-dish Pizza Pie, filled with savoury Italian sausage and layered in reverse, with the cheese on the bottom and the sauce on the top, is another creation entirely, of course. Different, yes! Which style of pizza is best? You, of course, are the judge.

Then there's the pasta . . .

PIZZA DOUGH

Makes 1 x 30cm/ pizza base

Multiply the quantities of this recipe and make a double or even a quadruple batch of dough, if desired – it freezes perfectly. Simply defrost at room temperature for 2 hours before use.

125g strong white bread flour, plus extra for kneading
½ sachet fast-action dried yeast (4g)
½ teaspoon caster sugar
¼ teaspoon sea salt
2 teaspoons olive oil, plus extra for oiling
Around 75ml water (see method)

- Place the bread flour, yeast and caster sugar in a large bowl. Mix well. Add the sea salt and mix again.

- Add the olive oil and mix once more. Slowly add around 75ml water, mixing thoroughly. Add a little more water as necessary to form a dough (the quantity can vary depending on brand of flour used, room temperature, etc.).

- Empty the dough out on to a well-floured work surface. Knead thoroughly for 3–4 minutes until smooth and then shape into a ball.

- Rub the bowl with a little olive oil. Return the dough to the bowl and cover with a wet cloth or oiled plastic wrap. Set aside for about 1 hour or until doubled in size.

- On a well-floured work surface knock the air out of the dough gently and form into a ball once again. At this stage the dough is ready for use, or it can be covered in plastic wrap and refrigerated for 24 hours (it will expand significantly), or freeze for up to 1 month.

PAN PIZZA

Serves 1

Starting the pizza off with direct heat from underneath guarantees a golden, crispy crust.

1 prepared Pizza Dough ball (page 159)
Olive oil
2 tablespoons Sweet Pizza Sauce (page 163)
75g mozzarella cheese, grated
Pepperoni, sweetcorn, fresh tomato, red onion, mushrooms, etc., to top (see Notes*)
Pinch of black pepper
Pinch of dried oregano

- Lightly grease a 25cm frying pan or crepe pan with a touch of olive oil. Knock the air out of the risen dough and shape the pizza using your hands or a rolling pin. When the dough is almost the same size as your prepared pan, carefully lift it on to the pan. Continue to flatten out, pressing into the corners until the entire pan is covered with dough.

- Lightly fork the surface of the dough (this prevents air bubbles as the pizza bakes). Cover the dough once more and set aside for at least 20 minutes and up to 1 hour.

- Spread the Sweet Pizza Sauce over the base of the pizza. Add grated mozzarella and any preferred toppings.

- Preheat the oven to 220°C/Gas 7. Place a large baking tray or pizza stone on the middle shelf of the oven.

- Place the pizza pan over a medium heat on the hob. Brush the outside of the crust with a little olive oil. As the heat builds, the pizza dough will begin to puff up a little. After 2–3 minutes, carefully lift the pizza up a little using a spatula and check the base for colour. If the pizza is sticking, continue cooking for a minute or so longer.

- After 3–4 minutes on the heat, the base of the pizza should have a nice golden colour. Carefully slide it off on to the baking tray/pizza stone in the oven and bake for 5–6 minutes or until the crust is crispy and the cheese has melted.

- Remove the pizza from the oven and garnish with black pepper and oregano whilst still piping hot. Allow to cool slightly, slice and serve.

Notes* Resist the temptation to add too many toppings to your pizza and allow the base to crisp up nicely. Onions, mushrooms, etc. can be added raw before baking, but should be sliced as thinly as possible.

SWEET PIZZA SAUCE

Makes enough sauce for 4 Pan Pizzas (page 161)

500ml passata
1 teaspoon olive oil
1 teaspoon garlic powder
1 teaspoon dried Italian herbs
1 teaspoon dried oregano
1 teaspoon sea salt
1 teaspoon caster sugar
Pinch of black pepper

- Place all the ingredients in a large saucepan. Bring to the boil, stirring often. Reduce the heat to low and simmer the sauce for 8–10 minutes.

- Set aside to cool completely, divide into 4 portions and store in the refrigerator for up to 3 days, or in the freezer for up to 3 months.

ITALIAN SAUSAGE

Serves 2 (Makes enough sausage for 2 Deep-dish Pizzas, page 166)

Perfect on pizza, in pasta or simply on its own, this fragrant Italian sausage is utterly delicious and takes just minutes to prepare and cook.

¼ teaspoon garlic powder
¼ teaspoon onion powder
½ teaspoon dried Italian herbs
Pinch of paprika
Pinch of dried chilli flakes
Pinch of dark brown sugar
Pinch of ground fennel seeds
½ teaspoon sea salt
¼ teaspoon black pepper
Pinch of white pepper
225g pork mince (not too lean, 15–20 per cent fat is ideal)
1 teaspoon apple cider vinegar
Olive oil for frying

- In a small bowl, combine the garlic powder, onion powder, Italian herbs, paprika, chilli flakes, brown sugar, fennel, sea salt, black pepper and white pepper. Mix well.

- Place the pork mince in a large bowl. Add the prepared spice mix and knead the spices into the meat until thoroughly combined. Add the apple cider vinegar and mix once more. Let the mixture stand for 5 minutes before use.

- To cook the sausage, heat 1 teaspoon olive oil in a heavy frying pan over a medium-high heat. Drop small pieces of the sausage mixture into the pan and cook, stirring occasionally, for 3–4 minutes or until the meat is charred, crispy on the edges and cooked through.

- Alternatively, using wet hands, roll the sausage mix into 8–10 small meatballs, arrange in a roasting tray and bake in a preheated oven at 180°C/Gas 4 for 15–18 minutes, turning once, or until golden and cooked through.

DEEP-DISH PIZZA PIE

Makes 2 pizzas (dough and sauce can both be frozen)

The original 'pizza pie', this dish is certainly more pie than pizza! Heavy on the tomato sauce, the crust is topped in reverse with cheese at the bottom and sauce on top.

200g strong white bread flour, plus extra for rolling out
2 tablespoons semolina
1 x 7g sachet active dry yeast
1 teaspoon sugar
½ teaspoon sea salt
2 tablespoons melted butter
About 120ml water
A little olive oil for greasing

Sauce
1 teaspoon olive oil
2 teaspoons salted butter
1 small onion, peeled and finely diced
2 x 400g tins chopped tomatoes
1 teaspoon dried Italian herbs
¼ teaspoon dried chilli flakes
¼ teaspoon ground fennel seeds
¼ teaspoon paprika
½ teaspoon sugar
½ teaspoon sea salt
½ teaspoon black pepper

To finish (per pizza)

100g grated mozzarella cheese

1 portion cooked Italian sausage (page 164)

30g Pecorino Romano cheese

- To make the dough, combine the white bread flour, semo-lina, yeast and sugar in a bowl. Mix well. Add the sea salt, melted butter and water; mix well once more until a dough has formed. Empty the dough out on to a floured work surface and knead for 3–4 minutes until smooth. Form into a ball, add a touch of oil to the bowl and place the dough back in the bowl. Cover with plastic wrap or a damp cloth and set aside until doubled in size, around 1–2 hours.

- When the dough has doubled in size, remove from the bowl, punch the air out of the dough a little, divide into 2 dough balls and knead each one again for 1 minute. Form into balls once more, cover again and set aside for 20 minutes. At this stage the dough may be covered and set aside in the refrigerator for a few hours before use, or cover in plastic wrap and freeze for up to 1 month.

- Meanwhile, make the pizza sauce. Heat the olive oil and butter in a small saucepan set over a low to medium heat. Add the diced onion and stir-fry for 2–3 minutes or until softened. Add the chopped tomatoes, Italian herbs, chilli flakes, fennel, paprika, sugar, sea salt and black pepper. Mix well and simmer for around 40–45 minutes, stirring occa-sionally, until the sauce has thickened. Once cooked, set aside to cool (the sauce may be made up to 48 hours in advance and stored in the refrigerator until needed or freeze for up to 1 month).

- Now, assemble the pizza. Preheat the oven to 200°C/Gas 6. Lightly grease a deep, round 23cm baking tin. On a floured surface, press out the dough until it's a little larger than the size of the tin. Carefully lift the dough into the tin and press out, pushing it completely up the sides of the tin to form a raised crust.

- Top the dough with the mozzarella cheese, followed by the Italian sausage, and finally, cover with the prepared sauce. Sprinkle Pecorino Romano cheese over the pizza, cover with foil and place the tin on a baking tray (this will help catch any spilled sauce – unlikely, but possible!).

- Bake in the centre of the oven for around 25 minutes, removing the foil after 10 minutes. Once cooked, allow the pizza pie to cool for 3–4 minutes before slicing and serving.

GARLIC KNOTS

Serves 2

Flour for rolling out
1 prepared Pizza Dough ball (page 159)
3 tablespoons olive oil, plus extra for greasing
3 garlic cloves, peeled and crushed
2–3 tablespoons Parmesan cheese, grated
1 teaspoon dried Italian herbs or dried parsley
½ teaspoon dried crushed chilli flakes
¼ teaspoon sea salt
Pinch of black pepper
Marinara Sauce (page 175), to serve

- Preheat the oven to 200°C/Gas 6. Meanwhile, roll the Pizza Dough ball out into a 20 x 20cm square. Cut into 10–12 strips. Tie each strip in a knot and arrange on a lightly greased baking tray.

- Bake the knots for around 12–14 minutes, or until crispy and golden.

- Meanwhile, place the olive oil, crushed garlic, grated Parmesan cheese, Italian herbs or parsley, crushed chilli flakes, sea salt and black pepper in a bowl. Mix well and set aside.

- When the knots are golden, remove from the oven and immediately brush generously with the prepared oil. Set aside for 2–3 minutes before serving with Marinara Sauce.

GARLIC TOAST

Serves 2

4–6 slices Country Bread (page 236) or French bread slices

Garlic Butter
1 teaspoon olive oil
4 tablespoons (60g) salted butter, softened
1 teaspoon garlic powder
½ teaspoon onion powder
½ teaspoon dried parsley
Pinch of sea salt
Pinch of black pepper
Pinch of white pepper

- To make the garlic butter, place the olive oil, salted butter, garlic powder, onion powder, dried parsley, sea salt, black pepper and white pepper in a bowl. Mix well until the butter is smooth. (At this stage, the butter can be covered and stored in the refrigerator for up to 1 week, if you wish.)

- To prepare the garlic bread, spread each slice of bread generously with the prepared garlic butter. Heat a dry frying pan over a medium heat. Carefully add the garlic bread slices to the pan, butter side down.

- Toast the bread in the pan for 2–3 minutes or until golden. Use a flat spatula to flip the bread and cook on the other side for a further 1–2 minutes before serving.

PENNE VODKA

Serves 2

200g penne pasta (dry weight)
1 teaspoon olive oil
1 small onion, peeled and finely chopped
60g pancetta, diced
1 garlic clove, peeled and crushed
Pinch of dried crushed chillies
4 tablespoons vodka
200ml passata
¼ teaspoon dried Italian herbs
4 tablespoons double cream
¼ teaspoon salt, plus extra to season
Pinch of black pepper
2 tablespoons grated Parmesan cheese, plus extra to serve

- Fill a large saucepan with water, season generously with sea salt and bring to the boil. Add the penne pasta, stir once and boil for 10–12 minutes (check the package instructions) or until al dente (firm to the bite). Drain, reserving about 1 tablespoon of the cooking water.

- Place the olive oil, chopped onion and pancetta in a frying pan set over a medium heat. Stir-fry for 2–3 minutes. Add the crushed garlic and chillies and stir-fry for a further minute.

- Stir in the vodka and continue cooking for 2–3 minutes, or until the vodka has reduced and cooked off. Add the passata and Italian herbs; simmer the sauce for another 2 minutes.

- Stir in the double cream, salt, black pepper and Parmesan cheese. Simmer for 1–2 minutes until the sauce is thick and creamy. Add the drained pasta, along with a little of the cooking water, mix well once more and serve topped with a little more Parmesan.

CHICKEN PARM

Serves 1

Crispy chicken, sweet Marinara Sauce, melting cheese ...
Middlesbrough in the north-east of England spawned the
legendary British fast-food version 'Chicken Parmo'. Here is
the American version.

100g plain flour
¼ teaspoon garlic powder
¼ teaspoon onion powder
¼ teaspoon dried Italian herbs (optional)
Pinch of cayenne pepper
¼ teaspoon sea salt
¼ teaspoon black pepper
1 egg
3 tablespoons milk
1 teaspoon Frank's Red Hot Sauce
1 skinless, boneless chicken breast fillet (125g)
Vegetable oil for deep-frying
2 tablespoons Marinara Sauce (page 175)
Small handful grated mozzarella cheese
1 tablespoon grated Parmesan cheese
Spaghetti in Marinara Sauce, to serve

- Place the plain flour, garlic powder, onion powder, Italian
  herbs (if desired), cayenne pepper, sea salt and black

pepper in a large bowl. Mix well and transfer to a large plate.

- Add the egg, milk and hot sauce to a large bowl. Mix well.

- Place the chicken breast on a large piece of greaseproof paper. Cover with another layer of greaseproof paper and use a meat hammer or heavy rolling pin to pound the chicken flat, around 5mm thick. Keeping one hand dry, dip the chicken in the egg and then in the seasoned flour. Dip the chicken back in the egg once more and finally in the seasoned flour to form a double breading.

- Heat the oil for deep-frying to 180°C/350°F. Preheat the oven to 180°C/Gas 4 too. Carefully place the breaded chicken in the hot oil and fry for 2–3 minutes, turning once, or until the chicken is cooked (the juices will run clear when pierced with a fork) and the breading is golden and crispy. Remove and set aside on a baking tray.

- Top the breaded chicken first with Marinara Sauce, then mozzarella cheese and finally, Parmesan cheese. Bake the cheese-topped chicken in the centre of the oven for 5–6 minutes or until the cheese is golden and melted. Serve with a simple side of spaghetti in Marinara Sauce.

MARINARA SAUCE

Serves 8

This sweet tomato sauce is extremely versatile and can be used as a pizza sauce or as a base for a variety of pasta dishes. Or ladle over Italian Sausage (page 164), top with mozzarella and bake at 200°C/Gas 6 for 8–10 minutes for a delicious side dish.

1 tablespoon olive oil
2 onions, peeled and finely chopped
4 garlic cloves, peeled and crushed
Pinch of dried crushed chilli flakes
2 x 400g tins chopped tomatoes or plum tomatoes
1 teaspoon sea salt
½ teaspoon black pepper
¼ teaspoon dried Italian herbs
1 teaspoon caster sugar (optional)

- Heat the olive oil in a large saucepan set over a medium heat. Add the chopped onions and cook, stirring often, for 5–6 minutes or until the onions are golden and have softened. Add the crushed garlic and chilli flakes and cook for a further minute.

- Add the tinned tomatoes, sea salt, black pepper and Italian herbs; mix well. Bring the sauce to the boil, immediately reduce the heat to low and simmer for around 1 hour or until thickened. Note that some tinned tomatoes are sweet enough after cooking but some remain a little acidic so taste your simmered sauce for sweetness and add sugar, if necessary.

- The sauce is ready to use immediately, or it can be cooled, covered and stored in the refrigerator for 2–3 days or in the freezer for up to 1 month.

EASY MAC'N'CHEESE

Serves 1–2

If diner food is simple comfort food, there's no better example of this than a classic Mac'n'Cheese. Indulgent and delicious, this recipe is also very easy to make. Good with Brisket (page 182) or Pulled Pork (page 184).

Sea salt to season
80g macaroni pasta (dry weight)
2 tablespoons double cream, plus extra as necessary
2 tablespoons milk, plus extra as necessary
50g mild Cheddar cheese, grated
2 processed cheese slices
Pinch of ground nutmeg
Pinch of cayenne pepper
Pinch of white pepper

- Bring a large saucepan of salted water to the boil over a high heat. When the water is boiling, add the pasta. Stir once and simmer for 7–8 minutes until just cooked (al dente, firm to the bite), or according to the packet instructions.

- Meanwhile, place the double cream, milk, Cheddar cheese, cheese slices, nutmeg, cayenne and white pepper in a small saucepan and set over a low heat. Stir gently until the cheese has melted and the sauce is smooth.

- Drain the cooked pasta, reserving just a little of the cooking water. Add to the warm sauce, stirring constantly and adding a little of the cooking water, if necessary. Stir over a low heat for 1–2 minutes or until the cheese sauce has slightly thickened and the pasta is thoroughly coated in sauce. Add a little more cream or milk if liked until the sauce reaches the desired consistency.

- Transfer the pasta to a serving dish or individual dishes and serve.

THREE-CHEESE MAC'N'CHEESE

Serves 2–4

280g macaroni pasta (dry weight)
2 tablespoons salted butter
1 tablespoon plain flour
450ml milk
½ teaspoon Dijon mustard
Pinch of cayenne pepper
Pinch of ground nutmeg
½ teaspoon sea salt, plus extra to season
Pinch of white pepper
150g medium-strength Cheddar cheese
2 slices of Monterey Jack cheese
2 tablespoons grated Parmesan cheese
Panko breadcrumbs and a little extra cheese to top
   (optional)

- Season a large saucepan of water with sea salt and bring to the boil over a high heat. When the water is boiling, add the pasta. Stir once and boil the pasta for 7–8 minutes until just cooked (al dente, firm to the bite), or according to the packet instructions.

- Meanwhile, melt the butter over a low heat in a separate large saucepan. Once melted, add the plain flour and mix well to form a roux or thick paste. Cook for 2–3 minutes, stirring, or until a nutty aroma fills the air. Add the milk a little at a time, whisking continuously until the sauce is smooth. Stir in the Dijon mustard, cayenne pepper, ground nutmeg, sea salt and white pepper. Mix well once more.

- Add the Cheddar cheese, Monterey Jack cheese and Parmesan cheese to the sauce. Mix well and simmer until the cheeses have melted and the sauce begins to thicken slightly. Add a little more milk if the sauce becomes too thick, or more cheese if too thin.

- Drain the cooked pasta, reserving just a little of the cooking water. Add the cheese sauce to the pasta and mix well. Check the Mac'N'Cheese for seasoning, adding more salt and white pepper, if necessary.

- Divide the Mac'N'Cheese between 4 individual oven-friendly serving dishes. Serve immediately, or top with Panko breadcrumbs and a little extra grated cheese and bake in a hot oven (200°C/Gas 6) for 5 minutes for a crispy topping.

6

MAINS

Whilst the huge array of side dishes and appetisers on diner menus is all too tempting, the main menu offers a variety of home cooking-style classics. Savoury meatloaf, topped with a deliciously sweet glaze, slow-cooked brisket, fall-apart, tender pulled pork, country-fried pork chops and crispy fish fry pieces are amongst the choices available. Served alongside creamy, buttery mashed potatoes and bright green broccoli, this is comfort food at its finest.

This chapter includes recipes for entrées that are bound to satisfy – the portion sizes are generous too, so you'll have plenty of leftovers to feed family and friends. Savoury, rich, indulgent and filling, these are full-on diner dishes you'll come back to for comfort, again and again.

BRISKET

Serves 6–8 depending on the weight of meat

This fall-apart tender meat makes a full meal alongside Mashed Potatoes (page 82) and Pan-steamed Broccoli (page 86), or it can be served French Dip sandwich-style (page 150).

1 tablespoon olive oil

2 onions, peeled and finely sliced

1kg beef brisket (cooking method and times will work for any brisket sized between 600g–1kg)

½ teaspoon sea salt

½ teaspoon black pepper

2 garlic cloves, peeled and crushed

450ml beef stock (or 1 beef stock cube mixed with 450ml boiling water)

1 tablespoon Worcestershire sauce

1 tablespoon oyster sauce

1½ teaspoons light soy sauce

1½ teaspoons dark soy sauce

¼ teaspoon white pepper

- Heat the oil in a heavy frying pan set over a medium heat. Add the sliced onions, mix well and fry for around 15–20 minutes, stirring occasionally, until the onions become golden.

- Preheat the oven to 180°C/Gas 4.

- Pat the beef brisket dry with kitchen paper, then season with sea salt and black pepper. Heat a dry heavy frying pan over a high heat and add the brisket. Fry for 3–4 minutes, turning a few times, until completely browned.

- Place the beef brisket in a large roasting tray, fatty side up, and top with fried onions. Add the crushed garlic, beef stock, Worcestershire sauce, oyster sauce, light and dark soy sauces and white pepper.

- Roast the brisket in the centre of the oven for around 3 hours or until tender. Remove from the roasting tray, slice or shred with a knife and fork and serve. Pour the cooked onions and brisket juices into a jug for use as onion gravy.

PULLED PORK

Serves 8

A diner classic, this slow-cooked pork spends the day cooking itself, leaving you free to prepare various side dishes! It freezes well in portions for up to 1 month.

1 tablespoon dark brown sugar
½ teaspoon cumin
¼ teaspoon cinnamon
¼ teaspoon smoked paprika
¼ teaspoon garlic powder
1½ teaspoons chilli powder
2 teaspoons sea salt
2.3kg boneless pork shoulder
2 onions, peeled and quartered
200ml chicken stock (from a cube or page 229)
3–4 tablespoons good-quality BBQ sauce to finish (or make your own, page 215)
Coleslaw, Potato Salad and Burger Buns (pages 106, 107 and 240), to serve

- Place the dark brown sugar, cumin, cinnamon, smoked paprika, garlic powder, chilli powder and sea salt in a bowl. Mix together well.

- Pat the pork shoulder dry with kitchen paper and rub with the prepared spices. Place the pork in a large dish, cover and set aside in the refrigerator for at least 2 hours or, ideally, overnight.

- Arrange the quartered onion pieces at the bottom of the slow cooker. Pour over the chicken stock and place the pork shoulder on top. Cover and cook on high for 2 hours. Reduce the heat to low and cook for a further 6–8 hours, or until the pork is fall-apart tender.

- Remove the cooked pork from the slow cooker. Pour the cooking liquid into a pot and set aside. Pull or shred the pork shoulder with a knife and fork, discarding any excess fatty pieces. At this stage the pork may be cooled and frozen in batches if desired (see Notes*).

- Return the pulled pork to the slow cooker, add a few table-spoons of the cooking liquid and as much BBQ sauce as you like. Mix well and cook on low for a further hour. Serve with Coleslaw, Potato Salad and Burger Buns.

Notes: To prepare the pulled pork in batches, freeze in portions at the stage indicated. To reheat from frozen, add 1 portion of frozen pulled pork to a large pot, cover with 250ml chicken stock and bring to the boil. Simmer the meat for 3–4 minutes or until defrosted and boiling. Drain the liquid, reserving around 1–2 tablespoons in the pot. Add 1 tablespoon of your favourite BBQ sauce and simmer the pork in the pan on a low heat for 3–4 minutes until caramelised and piping hot.

MEATLOAF

Serves 4–6

Over the years this American classic has developed a bad reputation, perhaps due to TV sitcom clichés as much as over-cooked offerings. In truth, it's comfort food at its best. Leftover sliced meatloaf, topped with a cheese slice and sandwiched in a burger bun, works well as a cheeseburger variation.

750g beef mince (not lean, around 15–20 per cent fat is
    ideal)
1 egg
1 onion, peeled and finely diced
275ml milk
150g Panko breadcrumbs
½ teaspoon dried mixed herbs
1 teaspoon parsley
1 teaspoon sea salt
½ teaspoon black pepper
Mashed Potatoes (page 82) and Brown Gravy (page 234),
    to serve

Glaze
4 tablespoons tomato ketchup (readymade or page 210)
1 tablespoon yellow (American) mustard
1 tablespoon soft brown sugar
1 tablespoon Worcestershire sauce

- First, make the glaze. In a small bowl, combine the tomato ketchup, yellow (American) mustard, soft brown sugar and Worcestershire sauce. Mix well and set aside.

- Now, prepare the meatloaf. In a large bowl, combine the beef mince, egg, diced onion, milk, Panko breadcrumbs, dried mixed herbs, parsley, sea salt and black pepper. Add 2 teaspoons of the prepared glaze. Use a fork to combine all of the ingredients, mixing until evenly distributed but no more.

- Preheat the oven to 180°C/Gas 4. Press the meatloaf mix into a lightly greased 900g loaf tin, pressing down with a fork to ensure the meatloaf is tightly packed into the tin. Place the tin on a baking tray and carefully cover the top of the meatloaf with the remaining prepared glaze.

- Bake the meatloaf in the centre of the oven for around 1 hour. If desired, tip halfway through cooking to drain away any excess fat. However, my personal recommendation would be that you leave it in for a better flavour. Serve with Mashed Potatoes and Brown Gravy.

Leftovers: Slice the cooled meatloaf, wrap tightly and store in the refrigerator for 2 days, or in the freezer for up to 3 months. To reheat, defrost completely in the refrigerator, heat a frying pan over a medium-high heat and add a touch of vegetable oil. Place a slice of meatloaf in the pan and fry for 3–4 minutes, turning occasionally. Add 1 tablespoon water to the pan, cover with a lid and cook for a further minute until piping hot.

SALISBURY STEAK

Serves 2

Meatloaf style-patties, topped with savoury onion and mushroom gravy.

250g beef mince
1 tablespoon Panko breadcrumbs
¼ teaspoon garlic powder
¼ teaspoon onion powder
Pinch of dried Italian herbs
Pinch of cayenne pepper
¼ teaspoon sea salt
¼ teaspoon black pepper
1 teaspoon tomato ketchup (readymade or page 210)
½ teaspoon yellow (American) mustard
½ teaspoon Worcestershire sauce
¼ beef stock cube, crumbled
1 teaspoon vegetable oil
1 teaspoon salted butter
½ onion, finely sliced
4 button mushrooms, quartered
1 teaspoon plain flour
250ml beef stock
Mashed Potatoes, Pan-steamed Broccoli and Dinner Rolls
(pages 82, 86 and 238), to serve

- Combine the beef mince, Panko breadcrumbs, garlic powder, onion powder, Italian herbs, cayenne pepper, sea salt, black pepper, tomato ketchup, mustard, Worcestershire sauce and crumbled beef stock cube in a large bowl. Combine thoroughly. Divide the mix in two and shape into oval patties.

- Heat the oil and butter in a heavy frying pan set over a medium heat. Add the prepared meat patties and brown for 3–4 minutes on each side until evenly coloured. Remove from the pan and set aside. Drain off any excess fat, leaving around 1 tablespoon in the pan.

- Add the sliced onion and quartered mushrooms and fry for 3–4 minutes. Add the plain flour and cook, stirring, for a further minute.

- Add the beef stock and mix well. As the stock begins to boil, return the meat patties to the pan and then reduce the heat to medium-low. Cover the pan loosely with a lid and cook for a further 15–20 minutes, basting the patties occasionally.

- Arrange the cooked patties on a serving plate and top generously with the onion and mushroom gravy. Serve with Mashed Potatoes, Pan-steamed Broccoli and Dinner Rolls.

CHICKEN FRIED STEAK

Serves 1

This famous Texas staple is said to have been invented by chance when a busy chef confused one order of fried chicken and one of steak to create this delicious hybrid! Despite the name, the dish contains only steak, breaded in a similar fashion to Chicken Fingers (page 67) – hence the name Chicken Fried Steak.

1 x 200–225g sirloin steak, trimmed of fat
1 egg
3 tablespoons milk
1 teaspoon Frank's Red Hot Sauce
4 tablespoons Panko breadcrumbs
4 tablespoons plain flour
¼ teaspoon garlic powder
¼ teaspoon onion powder
¼ teaspoon dried Italian herbs
¼ teaspoon paprika
¼ teaspoon sea salt
¼ teaspoon black pepper
Vegetable oil for frying
Biscuits or Mashed Potatoes (pages 44 and 82), to serve

Gravy
1 tablespoon vegetable oil
1 tablespoon salted butter

2 tablespoons plain flour
250ml milk
50ml chicken stock (from a cube or page 229)
¼ teaspoon sea salt
½ teaspoon black pepper

- Place the steak on a large piece of greaseproof paper. Cover with another layer of greaseproof paper and use a meat hammer or heavy rolling pin to pound the steak flat, around 5mm thick. Try to ensure the steak is as thin as possible. Set aside.

- Place the egg, milk and hot sauce in a large bowl; mix well.

- Mix the Panko breadcrumbs, plain flour, garlic powder, onion powder, Italian herbs, paprika, sea salt and black pepper on a plate.

- Fill a large frying pan one third full with oil. Heat to 180°C/350°F. Keeping one hand dry, dip the flattened steak in the plain flour (shaking off any excess), then into the egg, and finally, in the seasoned flour once more. Ensure the steak slice is evenly coated and place carefully in the hot oil. Fry for 2–3 minutes.

- Turn the steak and cook for a further 1–2 minutes, or until the breading is golden and crisp. Remove from the pan, drain off any excess oil and arrange on a baking tray. Set aside.

- Now, make the gravy. In a separate pan, heat the oil and butter over a medium heat. Once the butter has melted, add the plain flour and cook for 1–2 minutes. Add half of the milk, mixing well, until the mixture becomes smooth. Add the remaining milk, chicken stock, sea salt and black pepper. Simmer for 2–3 minutes or until the gravy becomes thick.

- Arrange the fried steak on a serving plate and top generously with gravy. Serve with Biscuits or Mashed Potatoes.

SLICED STEAK WITH GARLIC FRIES

Serves 1

225g beef sirloin steak
1 teaspoon vegetable oil
½ teaspoon sea salt
1–2 tablespoons beef stock (optional)
¼ teaspoon black pepper

Garlic-Butter Gravy
1 tablespoon salted butter
2 garlic cloves, peeled and crushed
1½ teaspoons plain flour
200ml chicken stock (from a cube or page 229)
Pinch of sea salt
Pinch of black pepper
Pinch of dried parsley
1 portion cooked French Fries (page 78), to serve

- Remove the sirloin steak from the refrigerator and rest on a plate at room temperature for 20 minutes before cooking.

- Heat a heavy frying pan over a high heat until just beginning to smoke. Rub the steak with vegetable oil and sea salt. Carefully place the steak in the hot pan and fry for 1 minute. Flip the steak and cook for a further minute.

- Reduce the heat to medium and continue cooking for a further 2 minutes on each side (rare), 3 minutes on each side (medium) or 4 minutes on each side (well done). If you prefer your steak well done, 1–2 tablespoons of beef stock added to the pan during the last 2 minutes of cooking time will help to keep the meat juicy.

- Finish the steak with a touch of black pepper and remove from the pan. Set aside on a plate loosely covered with foil to rest for 5 minutes.

- Whilst the steak rests, heat the butter in a small pan set over a medium heat. When the butter has melted, add the crushed garlic and cook for 30 seconds. Add the plain flour, whisking constantly. Cook the mixture for at least 1–2 minutes and keep whisking until the flour cooks out and a toasted/nutty aroma fills the air.

- Remove the pan from the heat and slowly add the chicken stock, whisking constantly. Return the pan to the heat, add the salt, black pepper and parsley. Simmer for 2–3 minutes or until the gravy thickens, adding a little more stock as necessary if it thickens too quickly.

- Slice the steak and arrange on a plate beside the French Fries. Cover the fries generously with Garlic-butter Gravy and serve.

CHILLI

Serves 4

This recipe may also be used to make Chilli-cheese Fries or Nachos (pages 79 and 64).

1 teaspoon vegetable oil

1 onion, peeled and finely chopped

1 garlic clove, peeled and crushed

1 red pepper, deseeded and finely chopped

½ green pepper, deseeded and finely chopped

500g beef mince

1 tablespoon tomato purée

1 tablespoon Worcestershire sauce

1 teaspoon cumin powder

½ teaspoon coriander powder

1 teaspoon chilli powder

½ teaspoon smoked paprika

½ teaspoon paprika

Pinch of sea salt

¼ teaspoon black pepper

400g tin chopped tomatoes

400ml beef stock

1 cinnamon stick

½ teaspoon dried oregano

1 square of good-quality dark chocolate (minimum 60 per cent cocoa solids)

400g tinned kidney beans, drained (optional)
Tortilla Chips (page 62), sour cream, guacamole and
    Pickled Jalapeños (page 225), to serve

- Heat the vegetable oil in a large saucepan set over a medium heat. Add the onion, garlic, red and green peppers. Fry for 3–4 minutes, stirring occasionally. Transfer the vegetables to a bowl and set aside.

- To the same saucepan, add the beef mince and cook for 2–3 minutes until evenly browned. Drain off any excess oil, add the tomato purée and Worcestershire sauce and cook for 2–3 minutes, stirring occasionally.

- Return the vegetables to the pan, add the cumin powder, coriander powder, chilli powder, smoked paprika, paprika, sea salt and black pepper. Mix well and cook for 1–2 minutes.

- Add the chopped tomatoes, beef stock, cinnamon stick and dried oregano to the pan. Bring to the boil, reduce the heat to low, cover and simmer for around 10 minutes. Remove the cinnamon stick, cover again and simmer for a further 20 minutes.

- Stir in the dark chocolate. Add the kidney beans, if desired, mix well and simmer for a further 15 minutes. Serve the chilli with Tortilla Chips, sour cream, guacamole and Pickled Jalapeños.

GREEN CHILLI

Serves 2

A lighter take on traditional chilli, the green chilli remains a fiery number – perfect for fans of spicy food. This dish uses tomatillos, which are part of the nightshade family. Despite the name, they are not tomatoes.

250g pork mince
½ onion, peeled and diced
¼ red pepper, deseeded and chopped
½ green pepper, deseeded and chopped
½ teaspoon jalapeño flakes (or 1 fresh jalapeño chilli, deseeded and chopped)
250ml chicken stock (from a cube or page 229)
1 teaspoon cornflour, mixed with 1 teaspoon water
380g tin of tomatillos (drained), or 7–8 fresh tomatillos
Small handful fresh coriander leaves, chopped
Pinch of cumin
Pinch of garlic powder
Pinch of dried oregano
Pinch of sea salt, plus extra to taste
Pinch of black pepper
Dash or two of lime juice
Sour cream and Tortilla Chips (page 62), to serve

- Heat a large dry saucepan over a medium heat. Add the pork mince, onion, red and green peppers. Mix well and cook for 2–3 minutes, or until the mince has browned. Drain off any excess oil, add the jalapeño flakes or chilli and cook for a further minute.

- Add the chicken stock and cornflour mixture and mix well. Bring to the boil, reduce the heat to low and simmer for 20 minutes, stirring occasionally.

- Whizz the tomatillos and fresh coriander in a blender until smooth and add to the saucepan. Add the cumin, garlic powder, dried oregano, sea salt and black pepper. Mix well and simmer for a further 30 minutes, stirring occasionally.

- Check the chilli for seasoning and add a little more salt and a dash or two of lime juice, as liked. Serve with sour cream and Tortilla Chips.

COUNTRY-FRIED PORK CHOP

Serves 1

3 tablespoons plain flour
3 tablespoons Panko breadcrumbs
½ teaspoon garlic powder
¼ teaspoon onion powder
Pinch of dried Italian herbs
Pinch of cayenne pepper
¼ teaspoon sea salt
Pinch of black pepper
1 egg
3 tablespoons milk
1 teaspoon Frank's Red Hot Sauce
200–225g boneless pork chop, trimmed of any excess fat
4 tablespoons vegetable oil
Country Gravy (page 231), to serve

- Place the plain flour, Panko breadcrumbs, garlic powder, onion powder, Italian herbs, cayenne pepper, sea salt and black pepper in a large bowl. Mix well and transfer to a plate.

- Add the egg, milk and hot sauce to a separate bowl; mix well.

- Place the pork chop on a large piece of greaseproof paper. Cover with another layer of greaseproof paper and use a meat hammer or heavy rolling pin to pound the pork flat, around 5mm thick.

- Heat the oil in a heavy frying pan set over a medium heat. Keeping one hand dry, dip the pork chop first in the seasoned breadcrumbs, then into the egg mix and finally once more in the breadcrumbs.

- Carefully place the breaded pork chop in the hot oil and fry for around 6–8 minutes or until crispy and golden. Remove from the pan, draining off any excess oil, and arrange on a serving plate. Serve with Country Gravy.

SHEPHERD'S PIE

Serves 4

I was surprised and delighted to come across this British classic on diner menus in New Jersey. As tradition dictates, shepherd's pie is made with lamb mince. If desired, beef mince may be substituted and the dish renamed Cottage Pie.

500g lamb mince
1 medium onion, peeled and finely chopped
1 carrot, peeled and finely chopped
¼ small turnip or swede, trimmed, peeled and finely chopped
1 tablespoon tomato purée
1 tablespoon Worcestershire sauce
½ teaspoon dried mixed herbs
1 teaspoon dried parsley
Pinch of sea salt
Pinch of black pepper
350ml chicken stock (from a cube or page 229)
1 teaspoon cornflour mixed with 1 tablespoon water
    (optional)
Double portion of Mashed Potatoes (page 82) to top (use
    4 large potatoes)
Pan-steamed Broccoli (page 86), to serve

- Add the lamb mince to a large pot and set over a medium-high heat (no oil is needed). Use a wooden spoon to break up the mince and fry for 2–3 minutes until browned. Drain off any excess fat. Reduce the heat to low, add the chopped onion, carrot, turnip or swede, tomato purée and Worcestershire sauce. Mix well and cook for 5 minutes, stirring occasionally.

- Add the dried mixed herbs, dried parsley, sea salt, black pepper and chicken stock. Bring to the boil, cover and simmer for around 45 minutes, stirring occasionally.

- After 45 minutes, check for seasoning and add more salt and pepper to taste. Increase the heat to high and boil the mix for 2–3 minutes to reduce down. If a thicker gravy is required, add the cornflour and water mixture. Mix well and simmer for 3–4 minutes.

- Preheat the oven to 200°C/Gas 6. Transfer the cooked mince to one large pie dish or 4 individual ones. Cover with mashed potato and use the back of a fork to create some texture in the mash (this ensures lots of crispy bits when the pie bakes).

- Bake the pie for around 15 minutes or until the potato topping is golden and crispy. Remove from the oven, set aside to cool briefly (around 5–10 minutes) and serve with Pan-steamed Broccoli.

BBQ CHICKEN

Serves 4

This shredded BBQ chicken also works well as a taco filling.

1 teaspoon garlic powder
½ teaspoon onion powder
¼ teaspoon ground ginger
½ teaspoon smoked paprika
½ teaspoon chilli powder
1 tablespoon soft brown sugar
½ teaspoon sea salt
¼ teaspoon black pepper
Pinch of white pepper
Pinch of cinnamon
6 boneless, skinless chicken thigh fillets (500g total
    weight)
1 tablespoon vegetable oil
100ml chicken stock (from a cube or page 229)
3 tablespoons good-quality BBQ sauce (or make your
    own, page 215)
1 teaspoon Frank's Red Hot Sauce
Coleslaw and Burger Buns (pages 106 and 240), to serve

- Place the garlic powder, onion powder, ground ginger, smoked paprika, chilli powder, soft brown sugar, sea salt, black pepper, white pepper and cinnamon in a bowl. Mix well. Coat the chicken thigh fillets with the dry spice mix, cover and set aside in the refrigerator for at least 2 hours, or, ideally, overnight.

- Heat the oil in a heavy frying pan set over a high heat. Place the chicken thighs in the pan and cook for 2 minutes. Turn and cook for a further 2 minutes.

- Reduce the heat to low, add the chicken stock and cover the pan with a lid. Simmer the chicken for around 15 minutes or until just cooked through (the juices will run clear when pierced with a fork).

- Remove the chicken thighs from the pan and set aside on a chopping board. Shred into small pieces using a knife and fork. Whilst you shred the chicken, increase the heat on the pan to high and leave uncovered. The liquid will reduce slightly.

- Return the shredded chicken to the pan. Add the BBQ sauce and hot sauce, mix well and cook for a further 10 minutes over a medium heat, stirring often until the sauce is thick, sweet and sticky. Serve the BBQ chicken with Coleslaw and Burger Buns.

FISH FRY

Serves 1

America's answer to fish and chips!

4 tablespoons plain flour
2 tablespoons cornflour
1 teaspoon sea salt, plus extra to season
½ teaspoon black pepper
2 pinches bicarbonate of soda
2 tablespoons vegetable oil, plus extra for deep-frying
350–400ml beer or lager
130g white fish fillet (haddock, cod or pollock)
Tartare Sauce (page 218), French Fries (page 78) and
    lemon wedges, to serve

- To make the batter, add the plain flour, cornflour, sea salt, black pepper and bicarbonate of soda to a large bowl. Mix together well.

- Add the vegetable oil and mix once more. Slowly add the beer or lager, whisking thoroughly, until the batter reaches the consistency of single cream.

- Heat the oil for deep-frying to 180°C/350°F. Slice the fish fillet into 3 pieces and pat dry with kitchen paper. When the oil is hot, dip each piece of fish in the batter, shaking off any excess. Place the fish fillets carefully in the hot oil and fry for around 5 minutes, turning once halfway through frying.

• Remove the crispy cooked fish from the pan. Drain off any excess oil on kitchen paper and season well with sea salt. Serve with Tartare Sauce, French Fries and lemon wedges.

CHEESE & ONION PIE

Serves 4–6

1 large onion, peeled and roughly chopped
400ml vegetable stock
300g Cheddar cheese, grated
½ teaspoon yellow (American) mustard
125ml milk, plus extra as liked
Generous pinch of ground nutmeg
Pinch of sea salt
Pinch of black pepper
Pinch of white pepper
Plain flour for rolling out
2 batches of Pie Crust (page 246)
1 egg, beaten
Garden Salad (page 109), to serve

- Place the chopped onion and vegetable stock in a large pot set over high heat. Bring to the boil and then simmer for around 10 minutes until the onions have softened. Drain and set aside to cool briefly.

- Preheat the oven to 160°C/Gas 3.

- Place the softened onions in a large bowl. Add the grated Cheddar cheese, mustard, milk, nutmeg, sea salt, black pepper and white pepper. Mix well, adding a little more milk as necessary to ensure the mix isn't too dry.

- On a lightly floured surface, roll out one batch of the Pie Crust as thinly as possible (around 5mm thick) to a length slightly bigger than a 20cm pie tin. Use the rolling pin to carefully lift the dough on to the pie tin, pressing gently into the edges until the dough is shaped into the tin. Cover the pastry with greaseproof paper and top with baking beans. Blind bake for 10–15 minutes until the edges are just a little golden and partially baked.

- Pour the prepared cheese and onion mix on top of the partially baked crust, spreading as evenly as possible. Roll out the remaining portion of Pie Crust as above. Cover the pie with the rolled-out dough, crimping the edges with a fork to form a seal.

- Brush the top of the pie with beaten egg and bake for around 40–45 minutes or until golden. Allow the pie to cool slightly (if you can resist!) before serving with a side of Garden Salad.

7

CONDIMENTS &
ESSENTIALS

There are literally thousands upon thousands of all-American diners across the United States, with New Jersey (often called 'The Diner Capital') boasting over 600 of them. With competition fierce, each must do what they can to stay one step ahead of the competition. In many cases, in-house sauces, salad dressings and pickles can make all the difference in ensuring customers crave your food specifically and aren't satisfied with anything less.

Diner chefs prepare their own ingredients wherever possible, for financial reasons as well as quality control. Cooking a fresh batch of essentials every few days ensures nothing is wasted, an important goal in both home and professional kitchens.

The recipes in this chapter include some essential sauces and salad dressings. Of course, your hungry diners will thank you for having made the effort to make these things from scratch. As a bonus, your bank balance will be grateful too!

TOMATO KETCHUP

Makes around 200ml

The cooking time means this recipe is a little indulgent unless being made in bulk, but the end result is so sticky, savoury and sweet that it makes it worthwhile. Keeps well, covered in a bowl in the refrigerator, for up to 1 week.

400g tinned chopped tomatoes
3 tablespoons water
3 tablespoons apple cider vinegar
1 tablespoon maple syrup
Pinch of turmeric
Pinch of cinnamon
Pinch of allspice
Pinch of cayenne pepper
Pinch of celery seed
Pinch of garlic powder
Pinch of onion powder
¼ teaspoon sea salt
Pinch of black pepper

- Combine all the ingredients in a large saucepan set over a medium heat. Mix together well.

- When the mixture begins to boil, reduce the heat to low and simmer, uncovered, for around 60–90 minutes, stirring occasionally, until the sauce has reduced and thickened.

- Blend until completely smooth, return to the pan and simmer for a further 10–15 minutes until further thickened. Set aside to cool completely and store, covered, in the refrigerator overnight before use.

TOMATO SALSA

Serves 8

Mexican oregano is an entirely different herb from the oregano typically found in Europe, with a mild liquorice and slightly citrus flavour. It is well worth obtaining from good Mexican grocery stores or online. This rich salsa, using tinned tomatoes, has a strong concentrated tomato flavour and is perfect with Tortilla Chips (page 62).

½ small onion, peeled and chopped
2 garlic cloves, peeled and crushed
1 jalapeño chilli pepper, deseeded and sliced
1 x 400g tinned chopped tomatoes
1 tablespoon lime juice
Pinch of cumin powder
Pinch of paprika
Pinch of dried oregano (Mexican oregano, if possible)
Pinch of caster sugar
Pinch of sea salt
Pinch of black pepper
Small handful fresh coriander leaves, finely chopped

- Place all the ingredients in a blender. Pulse the mixture briefly 4–5 times until combined, but still with a little texture.

- Cover the salsa and set aside in the refrigerator for at least 1 hour to bring out the flavours before serving. Any leftover salsa can be refrigerated, covered in a bowl, for 2–3 days.

FRESH TOMATO SALSA

Serves 1–2

This simple salsa is great served with Tortilla Chips (page 62) or on top of Breakfast Tacos (page 48).

1 small onion, peeled and finely chopped
2 teaspoons lime juice
2 salad tomatoes, deseeded and diced
Small handful fresh coriander leaves, finely chopped
Pinch of sea salt
Pinch of black pepper

- Place the chopped onion and lime juice in a bowl. Mix together well and set aside for 5 minutes. Add the tomatoes, coriander leaves, sea salt and black pepper. Mix well and set aside for 10 minutes at room temperature before serving to bring out the flavours.

- The fresh salsa will keep well in a sealed container in the refrigerator for 2 days.

SWEET BBQ SAUCE

Makes around 350ml

Serve with Chicken Fingers or Baby-back Ribs (pages 67 and 76).

360ml tomato ketchup (readymade or page 210)
1 teaspoon yellow (American) mustard
2 teaspoons maple syrup
1 tablespoon honey
3 tablespoons dark brown sugar
1 tablespoon orange juice
1 tablespoon Worcestershire sauce
1 teaspoon regular white (distilled) vinegar
¼ teaspoon garlic powder
Pinch of cayenne pepper
1 teaspoon sea salt
¼ teaspoon black pepper

- Place all the ingredients in a large saucepan. Mix well over a high heat until the sauce begins to boil. Reduce the heat to low and simmer for 25–30 minutes, stirring often, until smooth and thick.

- Allow the sauce to cool completely, cover and refrigerate. Store in the refrigerator for up to 1 month.

BLACK PEPPER MAYO

Serves 4

Use this slightly spicy mayo as a dipping sauce or with Crispy Chicken Burgers (page 124).

4 tablespoons mayonnaise
½ teaspoon black pepper
½ teaspoon fresh lemon juice

- Place the mayonnaise, black pepper and lemon juice in a bowl. Mix together thoroughly, cover and set aside in the refrigerator for at least 1 hour before use.

- The prepared black pepper mayo will keep well in a sealed container in the refrigerator for up to 1 week.

RANCH DRESSING

Serves 1

This mildly garlicky creamy salad dressing is excellent served on the side with Maple Buffalo Wings or Nashville Hot Chicken (pages 69 and 73). It keeps well, covered in a bowl in the refrigerator, for 2–3 days.

3–4 tablespoons milk
Dash of lemon juice
4 tablespoons mayonnaise
¼ teaspoon garlic powder
¼ teaspoon onion powder
¼ teaspoon dried dill
¼ teaspoon dried parsley
¼ teaspoon dried chives
Pinch of sea salt
Pinch of black pepper

- In a large bowl, combine the milk and lemon juice. Mix briefly and set aside for 5 minutes.

- Add the mayonnaise, garlic powder, onion powder, dill, parsley, chives, sea salt and black pepper. Mix together well, cover and set aside, covered, in the refrigerator for 1 hour before use.

TARTARE SAUCE

Serves 2

The perfect accompaniment to Fish Fry (page 205)! Keeps
well, covered in a bowl in the refrigerator, for 1–2 days.

4 tablespoons mayonnaise
1½ teaspoons lemon juice
1 teaspoon finely chopped onion
4 gherkin slices (dill pickles), finely chopped
Pinch of sea salt
Pinch of black pepper

- Place all the ingredients in a large bowl. Mix well, cover
  and set aside in the refrigerator for 1 hour before use.

REMOULADE

Serves 2

This American take on the classic French condiment is an essential part of the Po' Boy experience (page 152). It also pairs perfectly with Fish Fry (page 205).

2 tablespoons mayonnaise
½ teaspoon yellow (American) mustard
½ teaspoon creamed horseradish
1–2 gherkin slices (dill pickles), finely chopped
1 teaspoon pickle juice
Pinch of Cajun Seasoning (page 228)
Dash of lemon juice

- Place all the ingredients in a bowl. Mix together well, cover and set aside in the refrigerator for at least 1 hour before use.

- Keeps well, covered in a bowl in the refrigerator, for 1–2 days.

BURGER SAUCE

Serves 1

This simple burger sauce is excellent, naturally, on a Smashed
Burger (page 120), but also makes a delicious dip for French
Fries (page 78).

 2 tablespoons mayonnaise
 1 tablespoon tomato ketchup (readymade or page 210)
 1 teaspoon yellow (American) mustard
 Pinch of garlic powder
 Pinch of onion powder
 Dash of Worcestershire sauce

* Combine all the ingredients in a bowl; mix thoroughly.
  Cover and set aside in the refrigerator for at least 1 hour
  before use to bring out the flavours.

* Keeps well, covered in a bowl in the refrigerator, for 3–4
  days.

SRIRACHA MAYO

Serves 2

Sriracha hot sauce has become hugely popular in recent years, and with good reason. This vibrant, slightly sweet hot Thai sauce is made with chilli peppers, vinegar and garlic and adds a delicious kick to everything, from tacos to ramen noodle bowls. Serve on top of a Smashed Burger (page 120) or as a dip with French Fries (page 78).

4 tablespoons mayonnaise
1 tablespoon yellow (American) mustard
1 tablespoon sriracha hot sauce
Dash of lime juice

- Place all the ingredients in a large bowl and mix thoroughly.

- Cover and set aside in the refrigerator for at least 1 hour before use to bring out the flavours. The mayo keeps well, covered in a bowl in the refrigerator, for 1–2 days.

HOT SAUCE

Makes around 300ml

This sauce will keep well, covered, in the refrigerator for up to 1 week. Bring to room temperature before serving with Breakfast Tacos (page 48), or simply spice up eggs or any of your favourite dishes!

4 red Thai chilli peppers (Bird's eye chillies), deseeded
1 Ramiro pepper (sweet pointed red pepper), deseeded
8 garlic cloves, peeled and crushed, or 4 tablespoons garlic paste
2 tablespoons caster sugar
1½ teaspoons sea salt
Dash of fish sauce (optional)
200ml regular white (distilled) vinegar

- In a blender, place the Thai chilli peppers, Ramiro pepper, garlic cloves or paste, caster sugar, sea salt, fish sauce (if desired) and white vinegar. Blend until smooth.

- Transfer the blended sauce to a saucepan. Bring to a boil over a medium heat and simmer for 3–4 minutes or until slightly thickened. Cool completely and set aside in the refrigerator in a sealed container for at least 2 hours before use to bring out the flavours.

MUSTARD RELISH

Serves 1–2

It's hard to believe this delicious relish can be made with just three ingredients – make it in bulk in BBQ season! An essential part of the Jersey-style Ripper experience (page 131), it also goes well with Sliders and Smashed Burgers (pages 118 and 120).

7–8 gherkin slices (dill pickles), finely chopped (about 45g)
½ onion, peeled and finely chopped
2 teaspoons yellow (American) mustard

- In a bowl, combine the chopped gherkin slices (dill pickles), onion and mustard. Mix thoroughly. Set aside in the refrigerator for at least 1 hour before use.

- Keeps well, covered in a bowl in the refrigerator, for 1–2 days.

THE AMERICAN DINER SECRET

HONEY MUSTARD DIP

Serves 2

Serve with Chicken Fingers or French Fries (pages 67 and 78).

4 tablespoons mayonnaise
1 tablespoon mild honey
1 teaspoon Dijon mustard
½ teaspoon lemon juice
Pinch of sea salt
Pinch of black pepper

- In a bowl, combine the mayonnaise, honey, Dijon mustard, lemon juice, sea salt and black pepper. Mix thoroughly.

- Cover and set aside in the refrigerator for at least 1 hour before serving. Keeps well, covered in a bowl in the refrigerator, for 1–2 days.

PICKLED JALAPEÑOS

Serves 4 (1 x 500ml jar)

Serve with Nachos (page 64), or on top of a Smashed Burger (page 120).

4–5 jalapeño peppers
125ml water
125ml regular white (distilled) vinegar
1 tablespoon caster sugar
1 teaspoon sea salt
1 garlic clove, peeled and crushed
Pinch of dried oregano

- Rinse the jalapeño peppers and pat dry with kitchen paper. Slice into rings, deseed and set aside.

- To a large saucepan, add the water, white vinegar, caster sugar, sea salt, crushed garlic and dried oregano. Bring to the boil over a medium-high heat. Once the mixture begins to boil, stir well, turn off the heat and add the sliced chillies. Leave to cool for 10–15 minutes.

- Arrange the pickled jalapeños and vinegar in sterilised jars (see Note°) for long-term use, or cool completely, cover and refrigerate (use within a week).

225

Note: To sterilise jars, wash in soapy hot water, rinse well and arrange on a rack in a preheated oven (120°C/ Gas ½) for 15 minutes.

CARAMELISED ONIONS

Serves 2

Serve the onions on top of a Smashed Burger (page 120).

2 large Spanish onions
1½ teaspoons vegetable oil
1½ teaspoons salted butter
Pinch of sea salt

- Peel and slice the onions as thinly as possible. Heat the vegetable oil and butter in a large frying pan set over a medium heat. When the butter has melted, add the onions and mix well.

- Reduce the heat to medium-low and cook for around 10 minutes, stirring often. Add the sea salt, mix well once more and continue to cook for a further 15–25 minutes, or until the onions are golden and caramelised.

CAJUN SEASONING

Makes 4 tablespoons (12 portions, assuming 1 teaspoon per serving)

This spice blend works well as a rub with chicken or meat and is deliciously smoky when sprinkled over French Fries (page 78). Alternatively, use as a spice rub for a variation on Pulled Pork (page 184).

1 tablespoon smoked paprika
½ teaspoon paprika
½ teaspoon cayenne pepper
1 teaspoon dried thyme
2 teaspoons dried oregano
1 teaspoon ground fennel seeds
1 teaspoon garlic powder
1 teaspoon onion powder
1½ teaspoons sea salt
1 teaspoon black pepper
1 teaspoon white pepper

- Combine all the ingredients in a bowl. Mix thoroughly and set aside in a sealed container. The prepared spice mix will keep well in a cool dry place for up to 3 months.

CHICKEN STOCK

Makes around 1 litre, depending on the reduction

This frugal use of chicken bones rewards you with the most delicious stock. If you use organic vegetables, freeze the peelings and trimmings in a sealable bag for up to 1 month for use in other stocks too.

Note: This chicken stock is unseasoned – if using home-made chicken stock in recipes, add a generous amount of sea salt (around 1 teaspoon per 500ml of stock used). If using stock cubes for stock in recipes, adding further seasoning is unnecessary.

Leftover bones from 1 oven-roasted chicken (or
   equivalent)
1 small onion, peeled and quartered
2 garlic cloves, peeled and crushed
1 carrot, trimmed and sliced
1 celery stick, trimmed and sliced
2 bay leaves
8–10 black peppercorns

- Place all the ingredients in a large saucepan or casserole. Cover with water (around 2 litres) and bring to the boil over a high heat. Reduce the heat to low, cover with a lid and simmer for 3 hours.

- Sieve the bones and vegetables from the stock and return the liquid to the pan. Simmer for a further hour.

- At this stage the stock is ready to use. If desired, boil over a high heat for a further 30 minutes to reduce by half. This ensures the stock takes up less freezer space and the concentrated stock can be diluted 1:1 with water.

- The prepared stock keeps well, covered in the refrigerator, for 3–4 days and up to 3 months, covered in the freezer.

COUNTRY GRAVY

Serves 2–4

Serve over Biscuits or with Country-fried Pork Chops (pages 44 and 199).

3 tablespoons salted butter (or leftover fat from cooked bacon, etc.)
2 tablespoons plain flour
300–350ml milk, plus extra as necessary
¼ teaspoon sea salt
Pinch of black pepper

- Heat the butter or fat in a heavy frying pan set over a medium heat. Once melted, add the plain flour, whisking constantly. Cook the mixture for at least 3–4 minutes, whisking until the flour cooks out and a toasted/nutty aroma fills the air.

- Remove the pan from the heat and slowly add the milk, whisking constantly. Return the pan to the heat and add the salt and pepper. Simmer for 2–3 minutes or until the gravy thickens, adding a little more milk as necessary if it thickens too quickly.

SAUSAGE GRAVY

Serves 2

Sausage Gravy is a traditional Southern breakfast dish and the perfect salty, savoury topping for slightly sweet biscuits (page 44).

1 teaspoon vegetable oil
250g Breakfast Sausage, uncooked (page 40)
1½ tablespoons salted butter
2 tablespoons plain flour
350ml milk, plus extra as necessary
Pinch of sea salt
Pinch of white pepper

- Heat the vegetable oil in a large frying pan set over a medium-high heat. Carefully drop small pieces of the Breakfast Sausage mix into the pan. Fry for 5–6 minutes, turning occasionally, until fully cooked and crispy on the edges. Remove from the pan and keep warm.

- Reduce the heat to medium, add the salted butter to the pan and mix well. Once melted, add the plain flour, whisking constantly until the flour cooks out and a toasted/nutty aroma fills the air.

- Remove the pan from the heat and slowly add the milk, whisking constantly. Return the pan to the heat, add the salt and white pepper and simmer for 2–3 minutes or until the gravy thickens (add a little more milk as necessary if it thickens too quickly). Return the cooked sausage pieces to the pan and mix once more.

BROWN GRAVY

Serves 2–4

The oyster sauce in this recipe is entirely my own take and is, in all likelihood, not traditional (oyster sauce, of course, being Chinese in origin). Oyster sauce is a savoury, slightly sweet and thick sauce that pairs well with beef and so makes the perfect addition to gravy. Also delicious served over Disco Fries (page 79)!

2 tablespoons salted butter (or leftover fat from cooked bacon, etc.)
2 tablespoons plain flour
Around 250ml beef stock
Pinch of sea salt
Pinch of black pepper
1 tablespoon oyster sauce (optional)

- Heat the butter or fat in a heavy frying pan set over a medium heat. Once melted, add the plain flour, whisking constantly. Cook the mixture for at least 3–4 minutes, whisking until the flour cooks out and a toasted/nutty aroma fills the air.

- Remove the pan from the heat and slowly add the beef stock, whisking constantly. Return the pan to the heat, add the salt and pepper and simmer for 2–3 minutes or until the gravy thickens, adding a little more stock as necessary if it thickens too quickly. Add the oyster sauce, if desired, and mix once more.

8

BAKER'S OVEN

Whilst there's a world of comfort to be found in shop-bought burger buns, both in taste and convenience, you can't beat the aromas and textures associated with freshly baked breads. Of course, the very best diners function not only as a restaurant but also as a fully-fledged bakery, producing their own dinner rolls, pizza doughs and bread.

Although baked goods typically require time, the work involved is often minimal and so a little effort and patience is well rewarded. In the case of dinner rolls, a batch of freshly baked rolls can be on the table in little more than an hour!

COUNTRY BREAD

Makes 1 small loaf

This small bread loaf is a great introduction to bread making and the beautiful crust makes it ideal for toasting. If desired, the bread may be sliced and wrapped tightly in plastic wrap before freezing for up to 1 month.

75ml water
½ teaspoon dried active yeast
½ teaspoon caster sugar
120g strong white bread flour, plus extra for kneading
½ teaspoon sea salt
2 teaspoons olive oil, plus extra for greasing

- Place the water, yeast and caster sugar in a jug. Mix once and set aside for 5 minutes.

- To a large bowl, add the bread flour, sea salt and olive oil. Mix well. Add the yeast mixture and mix again to form a dough.

- Empty the dough out on to a floured work surface and knead for 3–4 minutes, adding a little more flour as necessary, until it is smooth. Lightly grease the bowl, return the dough to the bowl, cover with a clean damp cloth and set aside for around 2 hours or until doubled in size.

- Empty the dough back out on to the floured work surface and knock it back (gently press out the air and knead again for a further 1–2 minutes). Form the dough into a smooth round ball and place on a lightly floured baking tray. Cover once more and set aside for 45 minutes.

- Preheat the oven to 200°C/Gas 6. Lightly score the top of the loaf with a very sharp knife (if desired) and dust with a little extra bread flour. Place the tray in the centre of the oven and bake the bread for 10 minutes.

- Reduce the heat to 180°C/Gas 4 and continue baking for a further 30 minutes or until golden and crusty. Remove from the oven and set aside on a wire rack to cool completely before serving.

DINNER ROLLS

Makes 6

These rolls are so quick to make, perfect when time is short and carbohydrate cravings need to be fed!

60ml milk
30ml water
1 tablespoon salted butter, plus extra for greasing
125g plain flour, plus extra for kneading
1 teaspoon dried active yeast
1½ teaspoons caster sugar
¼ teaspoon sea salt

To Finish
1 tablespoon butter, plus extra softened butter, to serve

- In a small saucepan, combine the milk, water and salted butter. Heat over a low to medium heat for 2–3 minutes or until the butter has melted and the mixture is warm.

- In a large bowl, combine the plain flour, yeast, caster sugar and sea salt; mix well. Add the prepared liquid and mix well, adding a further 1–2 tablespoons water, if necessary, to form a dough.

- Empty the dough out on to a floured work surface. Knead for 3–4 minutes or until smooth, dusting with a little more flour as necessary. Return to the bowl, cover with a damp cloth and set aside for 15 minutes.

- Divide the dough into 6 equal pieces. Form each piece into a ball and place on a lightly greased baking tray, leaving a little space between each roll. Cover again and set aside for 30 minutes.

- Meanwhile, preheat the oven to 190°C/Gas 5. Bake the dinner rolls in the centre of the oven for 15–20 minutes or until golden. Whilst the rolls are baking, melt the butter. Remove the rolls from the oven and immediately brush with melted butter. Serve with extra softened butter.

Note: Any leftover rolls can be used the following day: simply dampen with a little water, wrap in kitchen paper and microwave on full power for 20–30 seconds before serving. Alternatively, freeze in plastic wrap for up to 1 month.

BURGER BUNS/HOT DOG ROLLS

Makes 8 large burger buns/hot dog rolls or 16 slider-style rolls (page 118)

450g strong white bread flour, plus extra for kneading
60g caster sugar
1 x 7g sachet fast-action dried yeast
2 tablespoons salted butter
1 egg
1½ teaspoons sea salt
225ml water
Vegetable oil for greasing
1 egg white, mixed with 3 tablespoons water
Poppy seeds or sesame seeds (optional)
1 tablespoon butter, melted

• Place the bread flour, caster sugar and yeast in a large bowl. Mix well.

• Heat the butter gently in a saucepan set over a low heat until just melted. Add the egg, sea salt and water. Mix well and slowly add to the dry ingredients in the bowl, mixing well until a dough is formed.

• Empty the dough out on to a floured work surface. Knead for 3–4 minutes until smooth, dusting with a little extra flour as necessary. Alternatively, use a mixer with a dough hook and mix for 3–4 minutes. Lightly oil the bowl, return the dough to the bowl and cover with a wet cloth. Set aside for around 2 hours, or until the dough has doubled in size.

- Divide the dough into 8 pieces for large burger buns, or 16 pieces for smaller, slider-style buns. Shape into rounds for burger buns, or stretch into hot dog rolls. Arrange on a lightly greased baking tray, leaving a little space between each roll for rising. Press down gently to flatten the dough a little. Cover with oiled plastic wrap and set aside at room temperature for around 1 hour, or until the dough has visibly risen.

- Preheat the oven to 190°C/Gas 5. Brush the tops of the rolls with the egg white/water mix and top with poppy seeds or sesame seeds, if desired. Bake in the centre of the oven for around 15 minutes or until golden. Remove from the oven and immediately brush with melted butter to glaze. Set aside on a wire rack to cool completely before use.

Note: The finished rolls will freeze well for up to 1 month. Alternatively, the prepared dough can be frozen and defrosted before continuing as above – ideal as it means you can enjoy fresh buns every day!

BAGELS

Makes 4 bagels

Nothing says New York better than a bagel and a *schmear* (spread)! These bagels will freeze well for up to 1 month.

175ml barely-warm water
2 teaspoons caster sugar
1 teaspoon active dry yeast
250g white bread flour, plus extra for kneading
¾ teaspoon sea salt
A little vegetable oil for greasing

- Place the water, caster sugar and yeast in a bowl. Set aside without mixing for 5 minutes. After 5 minutes, mix well.

- Place the bread flour and sea salt in another bowl. Mix well. Make a well in the centre and slowly add the yeast liquid, mixing until a dough has formed. Add a little more water, if necessary.

- Empty the dough out on to a floured work surface. Knead for 3–4 minutes until smooth, dusting with a little extra flour as necessary. Lightly oil the bowl, return the dough to the bowl and cover with a wet cloth. Set aside for around 1 hour or until the dough has doubled in size.

- Empty the dough out on to the work surface. Knock the air out (page 237) and knead again for 1 minute. Divide into 4 pieces and roll each one into a ball.

- Flour the handle of a wooden spoon and use it to poke a hole in the centre of each dough ball. Carefully manipulate the dough by hand to stretch the hole in the centre to around 5cm. As each bagel is prepared, set aside on a lightly greased baking tray.

- Cover the prepared bagels again and set aside for 20 minutes. Meanwhile, preheat the oven to 220°C/Gas 7. Bring a large pot of water to the boil.

- Carefully place 1 prepared bagel in the boiling water. Simmer for 1–2 minutes on each side (the longer the boil, the chewier your finished bagels will be). Remove the simmered bagel from the water using a slotted spoon and return to the greased baking tray. Repeat until all of the bagels have been in the water.

- Place the tray of bagels in the centre of the oven and immediately reduce the temperature to 200°C/Gas 6. Bake for 20 minutes or until crisp and golden. Serve warm or cool completely and then toast to serve with your favourite breakfast foods. Try classic 'Lox' with a generous spreading of cream cheese topped with salmon cured in a salt/sugar brine. Alternatively, use smoked salmon.

Variation: After the bagels have been simmered in water, brush with beaten egg and top with sesame or poppy seeds, as desired.

CORNBREAD MUFFINS

Makes 12

These muffins are simple and delicious served warm with Pulled Pork (page 184). However, you could also add some grated Cheddar cheese or cooked bacon pieces to the batter, if desired. Alternatively, brush the tops with honey immediately after baking for an added sweet finish.

250ml milk
1 tablespoon lemon juice
1 egg
4 tablespoons salted butter, melted
125g plain flour
125g cornmeal
5 tablespoons caster sugar
2 teaspoons baking powder
Pinch of sea salt
Melted butter or vegetable oil for greasing, or 12 paper muffin cases

- Preheat the oven to 200°C/Gas 6. Meanwhile, add the milk and lemon juice to a large jug. Mix once and set aside for 5 minutes. Add the egg and melted butter and mix once more.

- Place the plain flour, cornmeal, caster sugar, baking powder and sea salt in a large bowl. Mix well. Add the prepared liquids, whisking briefly until just combined – a few lumps are fine!

- Lightly grease a 12-cup muffin tray with melted butter or vegetable oil, or line with paper cases. Divide the cornbread batter between the tray or cases. Bake in the centre of the oven for around 15–20 minutes or until the tops are puffed up and golden. Cool slightly on a wire rack before serving.

- The muffins are best enjoyed fresh from the oven but will keep well for 1–2 days in a tin at room temperature.

PIE CRUST

Makes enough pastry for 1 pie crust (a double batch is necessary for double-crust pies with a pastry bottom and lid)

A good diner prides itself on its own house-made dishes and a good American pie needs a good pie crust. This recipe can be used for both savoury and sweet dishes (see Cheese & Onion Pie and Pecan Pie, pages 207 and 252).

    80g cold salted butter, cut into small pieces
    175g plain flour
    About 40ml water

- Place the cold salted butter and plain flour in a large bowl. With fingertips, rub the butter into the flour until a breadcrumb consistency is achieved.

- Slowly add the water, mixing constantly until a soft dough forms. Use a little less or more water, as necessary – the type of flour used, room temperature and other factors such as humidity can all affect how much water is needed.

- When the dough comes together, form a ball, cover in plastic wrap and set aside in the refrigerator for 20 minutes. The dough is now ready to use as per recipe instructions.

9

DESSERTS & DRINKS

Diner restaurants are cleverly laid out, enticing customers with open glass displays of all manner of cakes and sweet treats. Typically situated at the entrance or counter to ensure visibility, it's hard to resist finishing off a good meal with an indulgent dessert – particularly when the range of delicious delights is on display in front of your eyes!

Diner portion sizes are decidedly generous and so, of course, takeaway boxes are always available for 'to go' orders. This chapter includes classics like Pecan Pie and Key Lime Pie. Doughnuts, whilst undoubtedly excellent as a dessert item on any menu, are equally popular as a breakfast treat, served alongside a pot of freshly brewed coffee.

Savoury or sweet, a good meal needs something equally delicious to wash things down. Many diners have an extensive range of cocktails and mocktails and this chapter also includes recipes for some of those drinks. Who can resist an ice-cream soda float or a hot chocolate?

BLUEBERRY COBBLER

Serves 4–6

Cobbler dishes originated in the British-American colonies and were created as an alternative to suet pudding dishes due to a lack of ingredients. Necessity is the mother of invention after all!

4 tablespoons salted butter
120g self-raising flour
120g caster sugar
Pinch of sea salt
1 egg
180ml milk
125g blueberries (fresh or frozen)
1 teaspoon cinnamon
½ teaspoon ground nutmeg
Good-quality vanilla ice cream, to serve

- Preheat the oven to 160°C/Gas 3.

- Dot the butter in a large baking dish and place in the oven for 2–3 minutes until melted.

- To make the batter, add the self-raising flour, caster sugar and sea salt to a large bowl. Mix well. Add the egg and milk to a separate bowl; mix well. Now, add the egg/milk mixture to the dry ingredients and mix until just combined.

- In another bowl, combine the blueberries, cinnamon and nutmeg. Mix well.

- Pour the batter into the baking dish on top of the melted butter. Add the prepared fruit mix, without stirring, and place the dish in the centre of the oven. Bake for 40–45 minutes until the pie has risen and the batter has turned golden brown.

- Remove the cobbler from the oven and allow to cool for 10 minutes – the butter from the bottom of the dish will be soaked up into the cobbler as it cools slightly.

- Serve warm with vanilla ice cream. Any leftover cobbler will keep, covered, at room temperature for 2 days.

CHERRY PIE

Serves 8

What could be more American than cherry pie? This recipe is worth the time it takes to pit the fresh cherries. However, tinned could be used, if desired – drain well to avoid excess liquid in the baked pie.

1kg fresh cherries, pitted
100g caster sugar
50g dark brown sugar
1 teaspoon cinnamon
2 tablespoons cornflour
1 teaspoon lemon juice
1 teaspoon water
Dash of vanilla extract
Pinch of sea salt
Plain flour for rolling out
2 prepared batches Pie Crust (page 246)
1 egg
Good-quality vanilla ice cream, to serve

- Preheat the oven to 200°C/Gas 6.

- Place the cherries, caster sugar, dark brown sugar, cinnamon, cornflour, lemon juice, water, vanilla extract and sea salt in a large bowl. Mix thoroughly.

- Lightly flour a work surface and roll out the first batch of Pie Crust to line a 23cm baking tin. Carefully spoon the prepared cherry mix over the crust. Roll out the second batch of Pie Crust and lay carefully over the filling. With your fingertips, crimp the edges to form a seal between the bottom and top Pie Crust.

- Whisk the egg and brush the top of the pie generously to glaze. Place the pie dish on a baking tray in the centre of the oven and bake for 20 minutes. Reduce the heat to 180°C/Gas 4 and bake for a further 30–35 minutes or until the pastry is golden.

- Remove the pie and set aside to cool on a rack for at least 2–3 hours. Slice and serve with good-quality vanilla ice cream.

PECAN PIE

Serves 6

Whilst the origins of Pecan Pie are debatable, pecans them-selves are native to the southern United States. Evidence indicates this ingredient was used by Native Americans over 8,000 years ago.

220g caster sugar
80g golden syrup
80g dark brown sugar
50ml water
3 eggs
70g salted butter
Dash of vanilla extract
100g chopped pecan nuts (and more for decoration, if desired)
Plain flour for rolling out
1 portion of Pie Crust (page 246)
Good-quality vanilla ice cream, to serve

• Preheat the oven to 160°C/Gas 3.

• Place the caster sugar, golden syrup, dark brown sugar and water in a large saucepan. Bring to the boil over a medium heat. When the mixture boils, remove from the heat and set aside.

- In a large bowl, whisk the eggs briefly until combined.

- Add the salted butter and the vanilla extract to the prepared sugar mix. Once the butter has melted into the sugar, slowly pour the mix into the eggs, whisking constantly to ensure the eggs don't begin to scramble. Add the chopped pecans and mix once more.

- On a lightly floured work surface, roll out the Pie Crust as thinly as possible (around 5mm thick) to a length slightly bigger than a 20cm pie tin. Use the rolling pin to carefully lift the dough on to the pie tin, pressing gently into the edges until the dough is shaped into the tin. Cover the pastry with greaseproof paper and top with baking beans. Blind bake for 10–15 minutes until the edges are just a little golden and partially baked.

- Pour the pie filling into the partially baked pastry crust. Lightly scatter some extra chopped pecan nuts over the top of the pie, if desired.

- Bake the pie in the centre of the oven for 50–60 minutes, or until it begins to darken slightly and a flaky crust forms. Remove from the oven and set aside on a wire rack to cool completely before serving with ice cream.

BANANA CREAM PIE

Serves 6

Dulce de leche (literally translated from Spanish as 'candy of milk') is made by slowly heating sweetened milk to create a substance with a caramel quality. It is now widely available in supermarkets.

Plain flour for rolling out
1 portion of Pie Crust (page 246)
100g dulce de leche (Carnation® Caramel)
2 large bananas, peeled and sliced
300ml milk
Dash of vanilla extract
3 egg yolks
120g caster sugar
25g self-raising flour
25g cornflour
Pinch of cinnamon
Pinch of ground nutmeg
250ml whipping cream

- Preheat the oven to 160°C/Gas 3. Meanwhile, roll the Pie Crust out as thinly as possible (about 5mm thick) on to a lightly floured work surface to a length slightly bigger than a 20cm pie tin. Use the rolling pin to carefully lift the dough on to the pie tin, pressing gently into the edges until the dough is shaped into the tin.

- Cover the pastry with greaseproof paper and top with baking beans. Blind bake for 10–15 minutes until the edges are just a little golden and partially baked. Remove the beans and greaseproof and bake for a further 15–20 minutes or until golden and fully baked. Set the baked Pie Crust aside to cool.

- Pour the dulce de leche or Carnation® Caramel into the pie crust. Layer the bananas on top and set aside.

- Pour 250ml of the milk into a large saucepan, reserving 50ml. Stir in the vanilla extract and bring to the boil over a medium heat. Once the mixture boils, turn off the heat.

- Add the remaining 50ml milk to a large bowl. Add the egg yolks, caster sugar, self-raising flour, cornflour, cinnamon and ground nutmeg. Slowly add the hot milk, whisking thoroughly to ensure the mixture doesn't split. Once fully combined, return the mixture to the saucepan. Bring to the boil once again, reduce the heat to low and whisk constantly for 4–5 minutes or until beginning to thicken. Pour the cooked custard into a bowl, cover with greaseproof paper and set aside to cool completely.

- Once the custard is cool, spoon generously over the sliced bananas until the whole pie is covered. Cover the pie in plastic wrap and set aside in the refrigerator for 2–3 hours until completely cool.

- In a separate bowl, whip the cream until stiff peaks form. Use a palette knife to spread over the top of the pie and serve.

THE AMERICAN DINER SECRET

KEY LIME PIE

Serves 6

This classic pie comes from the Key West district of Florida and traditionally uses key limes. Regular limes may be used, with equally zingy and zesty results.

100g shortbread
100g biscuits (Digestives, Hobnobs or Rich Tea)
100g salted butter, melted
2 x 400g tins of condensed milk
100ml double cream
150ml freshly squeezed lime juice
2 teaspoons finely grated lime zest
Whipped cream and thin slices of lime, to serve

- Preheat the oven to 160°C/Gas 3.

- To crush the shortbread and biscuits, place in a plastic bag. Secure the bag and tap gently with a rolling pin to form crumbs. Transfer to a large bowl.

- Add the melted butter and mix well. Transfer the mixture to a 20cm quick-release springform cake tin and press down into the base and the sides of the tin with your fingertips to form a biscuit crust.

- To a separate large bowl, add the condensed milk, double cream, lime juice and zest. Mix well and pour carefully over the top of the prepared biscuit layer.

- Bake the pie in the centre of the oven for around 5–8 minutes, or until bubbles form on the top. Remove from the oven and set aside to cool completely. Once cooled, refrigerate for 2–3 hours or until completely chilled.

- To serve, remove the pie from the tin, slice and serve with whipped cream and thin slices of lime.

CINNAMON PIZZA STICKS

Serves 2

Cinnamon flavoured desserts are hugely popular with diner-goers. This sweet take on pizza, perfectly paired with a smooth white icing dip, is one of the best examples. Whilst home ovens can't get close to the extreme heats found in commercial or wood-burning ovens, a heavy pizza stone preheated in the oven at full temperature for 1 hour before baking provides a good alternative and helps to ensure the crust bakes to golden, crispy perfection.

Vegetable oil for greasing
Plain flour for rolling out
1 prepared Pizza Dough ball (page 159)
2 tablespoons salted butter, melted
4–6 tablespoons Cinnamon Sugar (page 264)
White icing dipping sauce (page 265), to serve

• Lightly grease a 25cm frying pan or crepe pan with a little vegetable oil. On a floured surface, knock the air out of the risen dough (page 237) and shape the pizza using your hands or a rolling pin. When the dough is almost the same size as your prepared pan, use a rolling pin to carefully lift it on to the pan and continue to flatten out, pressing the dough into the corners of the pan until the entire pan is covered with dough.

- Use a fork to lightly prick holes across the surface of the dough (this prevents air bubbles as the pizza bakes). Cover with a tea towel and set aside for 20 minutes.

- Brush the dough generously with melted butter. Sprinkle half of the Cinnamon Sugar over the top.

- Preheat the oven to 220°C/Gas 7. Arrange a large baking tray or pizza stone in the middle shelf of the oven. Place the frying pan or crepe pan over a medium heat. As the heat builds, the dough will begin to puff up a little. After 2–3 minutes, lift the pizza up a little and check the base for colour. If the pizza doesn't want to lift, continue cooking for a little longer.

- After 3–4 minutes on the heat, the base of the pizza should have a nice golden colour. Carefully slide the pizza off on to the baking tray/pizza stone in the oven and bake for 5–6 minutes, or until the crust is crispy and the Cinnamon Sugar mix is bubbling.

- Remove the pizza from the oven and cover with the remaining cinnamon sugar whilst piping hot. Cool slightly before slicing into sticks and serve with white icing dipping sauce.

CINNAMON ROLLS

Makes 9

3 tablespoons salted butter, melted
3 tablespoons caster sugar
1 egg
Dash of vanilla extract
325g strong white bread flour, plus extra for kneading
175ml milk
1 x 7g sachet dried active yeast
Vegetable oil for greasing
Cream Cheese Frosting (page 267), to decorate

Filling
60g dark brown sugar
60g soft brown sugar
1 heaped tablespoon cinnamon powder
60g salted butter, softened

- Place the melted butter, caster sugar, egg, vanilla extract and bread flour in a bowl. Mix briefly.

- Warm the milk gently for 2–3 minutes in a small saucepan set over a low heat. Add the yeast to the warm milk, mix once and add to the prepared flour, stirring until a dough has formed.

- Empty the dough out on to a floured work surface and knead for 10 minutes (this step can be made easier by using a food mixer with a dough hook). Once the dough is smooth, form a ball, place in a lightly greased bowl, cover with a clean damp cloth and set aside for around 2 hours or until doubled in size.

- Now, prepare the filling. To a large bowl, add dark brown sugar, soft brown sugar, cinnamon powder and salted butter. With your fingertips, rub the butter into the sugar until the mix takes on a breadcrumb-like texture.

- Empty the dough back on to the floured work surface. Roll out to around 35 x 25cm. Cover the surface of the dough with the prepared sugar-cinnamon mix, leaving a little space around the edges to ensure the dough is easy to roll.

- Roll the dough tightly from the short end to form a Swiss roll shape. Use a sharp knife to slice the roll into 9 equal pieces. Arrange the sliced pieces in a greaseproof-lined 25cm cake tin with the filling facing up (leave a little space between each cinnamon roll as they will expand further as they rest).

- Cover the cinnamon rolls again and set aside for a further 30 minutes.

- Meanwhile, preheat the oven to 180°C/Gas 4. Bake the cinnamon rolls for around 25 minutes or until browned around the sides. Once baked, leave to cool slightly before topping with Cream Cheese Frosting. Serve whilst still warm or set aside to cool completely.

DOUGHNUTS

Makes 12

2 tablespoons warm water
1 x 7g sachet dried active yeast
190ml milk
1 egg
60g salted butter, melted
450g plain flour, plus extra for kneading
60g caster sugar
Vegetable oil for greasing and deep-frying
Cinnamon Sugar, or Vanilla White Icing Glaze or
    Chocolate Glaze (pages 264, 265 and 266), if desired
Grated chocolate, hundreds and thousands or chopped
    nuts to garnish, if desired

- Place the warm water and dried active yeast in a large bowl.
  Mix briefly and set aside for 5 minutes.

- Heat the milk in a saucepan set over a medium heat for 3–4
  minutes until warm. Set aside for 5 minutes, then add the
  egg and mix well. Stir in the melted butter.

- Place the plain flour and caster sugar in a large bowl. Add
  the prepared liquids and mix well until a dough has formed.

- Empty the dough out on to a floured work surface. Knead
  for 3–4 minutes, dusting with a little extra flour as

necessary, until smooth. Place the dough in a lightly greased bowl, cover with a clean damp cloth and set aside for around 2 hours or until the dough has doubled in size.

- Place the dough back on a floured work surface. Gently press it down with your hands and roll out to a thickness of around 1–1¼cm. Use a doughnut cutter to cut 12 dough-nuts or use a scone/biscuit cutter or the top of a jam jar to cut rounds. Push holes in the centre of each one with the floured handle of a wooden spoon.

- Set the doughnuts on a lightly floured tray or work surface, cover again with a damp cloth and set aside for around 45 minutes or until puffed up.

- Heat the oil for deep-frying to 180°C/350°F. Use tongs to carefully place the doughnuts in the fryer in batches. Fry for 40–50 seconds on each side or until golden (use chop-sticks to easily flip the doughnuts in the oil during cooking).

- Remove the doughnuts from the pan, drain off any excess oil on kitchen paper and arrange on a wire rack. Whilst still warm, top with Cinnamon Sugar, or your favourite glaze and garnish as liked (above).

CINNAMON SUGAR

Makes about 100g

Works well with Doughnuts (262) and French Toast Sticks (page 17).

100g caster sugar
2 teaspoons cinnamon

- In a bowl, mix together the caster sugar and cinnamon. Keeps well in a sealed container in a cool, dry place for up to 1 month.

VANILLA WHITE ICING GLAZE

Makes enough glaze for 6 doughnuts

Made thick, this glaze is perfect for topping doughnuts (page 262) and will set nicely. Alternatively, add a little more milk to create a white icing dipping sauce that goes perfectly with Cinnamon Pizza Sticks (page 258).

225g icing sugar
About 3 tablespoons milk
Dash of vanilla extract

- To a large bowl, add the icing sugar, milk and vanilla extract. Mix thoroughly, adding a drop or two more of milk, if necessary, until the glaze has thickened but can still be poured.

CHOCOLATE GLAZE

Makes enough for 6 doughnuts

For a chocolate orange doughnut, you could add a dash of orange essence to this glaze with good effect.

100g icing sugar
25g cocoa powder
Dash of vanilla extract
About 2 tablespoons milk

- Place the icing sugar, cocoa powder and vanilla extract in a bowl. Mix well. Slowly add the milk, whisking constantly, until the glaze has thickened but can still be poured.

CREAM CHEESE FROSTING

Makes enough frosting for 9 cinnamon rolls

Delightfully decadent, spread this Cream Cheese Frosting over Cinnamon Rolls (page 260) to your heart's content! The frosting also pairs well with all manner of cakes, cupcakes, pancakes and doughnuts.

   100g cream cheese
   50g butter, softened
   1 teaspoon vanilla extract
   300g icing sugar

- To a large bowl, add the cream cheese, softened butter, vanilla extract and icing sugar. Mix thoroughly until the frosting is smooth and no lumps of butter remain.

STRAWBERRY CHOCOLATE WAFFLES

Makes 4

Any leftover waffles will keep well in a food bag or storage container at room temperature for up to 2 days. They also freeze well. Reheat under the grill or in the toaster before serving.

100g plain flour
2 tablespoons caster sugar
1 tablespoon cocoa powder
Pinch of bicarbonate of soda
2 tablespoons chocolate chips
150ml milk
1 tablespoon butter, melted
1 egg
A little vegetable oil
Freshly sliced strawberries, chocolate chips, marshmallows, whipped cream and Chocolate Syrup (page 271), to serve

- In a large bowl, combine the plain flour, caster sugar, cocoa powder, bicarbonate of soda and chocolate chips Mix well.

- In a separate bowl or jug, combine the milk and melted butter. Mix well. Add the egg to the milk and butter and mix well once more. Add the liquid mixture to the dry ingredients and mix until just combined – a few lumps are fine.

- Spoon the waffle batter into a lightly greased and preheated waffle iron and cook according to the manufacturer's instructions, usually around 5–7 minutes. If desired, the cooked waffles may be kept warm on a rack in the oven at the lowest available temperature whilst the remaining waffles are cooked.

- To serve, place a chocolate waffle on a serving plate. Garnish with freshly sliced strawberries, chocolate chips and marshmallows. Add whipped cream and finish off with Chocolate Syrup.

CHOCOLATE PUDDINGS

Serves 2

3 tablespoons caster sugar
2 tablespoons cocoa powder
1½ tablespoons cornflour
Pinch of sea salt
225ml milk
Dash of vanilla extract (optional)
Whipped cream, chocolate chips and Chocolate Syrup
    (page 271), to serve

- Place the caster sugar, cocoa powder, cornflour and sea salt in a saucepan; mix well. Add the milk and heat the mixture over a medium heat, stirring often.

- When the mixture begins to boil, reduce the heat to medium-low and simmer for 3–4 minutes, stirring often, until the mixture becomes smooth and begins to thicken. Add a dash of vanilla extract, if desired, mix well and turn off the heat.

- Divide the pudding mix between 2 heavy serving bowls or glasses. Allow to cool for 20 minutes then refrigerate for 2–3 hours or until completely set.

- When ready to serve, garnish the puddings with whipped cream, sprinkle with chocolate chips and finish off with Chocolate Syrup.

CHOCOLATE SYRUP

Makes around 400ml

This syrup will thicken a little more as it sits in the refrigerator and is the perfect accompaniment to Strawberry Chocolate Waffles (page 268) and Chocolate Chip Pancakes (page 12).

250ml water
175g caster sugar
60g cocoa powder
Pinch of sea salt
Dash of vanilla extract

- Place the water and caster sugar in a large saucepan and set over a medium heat. Mix well, bring to the boil and then reduce the heat. Simmer for 1 minute until the sugar has dissolved.

- Stir in the cocoa powder, sea salt and vanilla extract. The sauce will look lumpy at first but becomes smooth again as the cocoa melts. Simmer for a further 5–6 minutes, stirring often, until the sauce thickens slightly.

- Set the sauce aside to cool completely then pour into a squeezy bottle. The syrup can be stored in the refrigerator for up to 2 weeks.

BLOODY MARY

Serves 1

This famous 'hair of the dog' hangover cure can be made 'Virgin Mary' style without the vodka, if desired.

7–8 ice cubes
50ml vodka, chilled
225ml tomato juice, chilled
Juice of ½ lemon or lime
Dash of Tabasco sauce
Dash of Worcestershire sauce
Pinch of celery salt
Pinch of black pepper
Celery stick and a slice of lemon or lime, to garnish

- To a tall glass, add 5 or 6 ice cubes. Add the chilled vodka, tomato juice, lemon or lime juice, Tabasco sauce, Worcestershire sauce, celery salt and black pepper. Mix thoroughly.

- Top up the glass with more ice, garnish with the celery stick and a slice of lemon or lime and serve.

MARGARITA

Serves 1

40ml freshly squeezed lime juice
½ teaspoon sea salt
40ml Tequila
20ml Cointreau
Handful of ice cubes
Lime wedge, to garnish

- Rub a martini glass with about 1 teaspoon of the lime juice. Sprinkle the sea salt on to a plate and turn the glass in the salt so that it sticks to the juice and forms a layer around the rim of the glass.

- In a cocktail shaker, place the Tequila, Cointreau and the remaining lime juice. Add ice cubes and shake thoroughly for 20–30 seconds. Pour the margarita into the prepared glass carefully and serve with a lime wedge garnish.

THE AMERICAN DINER SECRET

ICE-CREAM SODA FLOAT

Serves 1

These fizzy, foamy ice-cream drinks are a delicious double indulgence.

330ml cola
1–2 scoops vanilla ice cream
Straws, to serve

- Pour 200ml of the cola into a tall glass. Add 1–2 scoops of ice cream. Top with the remaining cola, add straws and serve.

HOT CHOCOLATE

Serves 1

1½ teaspoons good-quality cocoa powder
1½ teaspoons caster sugar
1 tablespoon water
½ cinnamon stick
230ml milk
1 tablespoon double cream
Dash of vanilla extract
Grated dark chocolate and marshmallows (optional), to
    serve

- Place the cocoa powder, caster sugar and water in a bowl. Mix well to form a paste.

- Place the cinnamon stick, milk and double cream in a saucepan set over a medium heat. Warm through until the mix just comes to a boil. Quickly sieve into the bowl with the prepared cocoa paste and mix well. Add the vanilla extract and mix once more.

- Transfer to a mug. Top with grated dark chocolate and a sprinkling of marshmallows, if desired, and serve.

INDEX

breaded king prawns 65–6
po' boy 152–3

quesadilla
chicken quesadilla 88–9
pizza quesadilla 90

Rachel sandwich 144
ranch dressing 217
recipes using 67–70, 109,
112–13
red pepper
chicken philly 136–7
chicken quesadillas 88–9
chilli 195–6
Denver omelette 33–4
green chilli 197–8
macaroni salad 114–15
pimento cheese 63
refried beans 46–7, 64
relish, mustard 107–8, 131,
150–1, 223
remoulade 219
recipes using 65–6, 152–3
Reuben sandwich 144
ribs, baby-back 76–7
rippers, Jersey-style 131, 223
Roquefort cheese, Cobb salad
112–13

salads 91–115
Caesar salad 110–11
Cobb salad 112–13
coleslaw 106

garden salad 109, 207–8
macaroni salad 114–15
potato salad 107–8, 184–5
Salisbury steak 188–9
salmon, smoked, eggs royale 30
salsa
fresh tomato 48, 64, 214
tomato 212–13
sandwiches 117
BLT 138
cheesesteak 134–5
chicken philly 136–7
French dip 150–1
grilled cheese sandwich
104–5, 139–40
hot turkey sandwich 145
Monte Cristo sandwich
146–7
patty melt 141–2
Rachel sandwich 144
Reuben sandwich 144
Taylor ham, egg & cheese
148–9
tuna melt 143
sauces
blueberry 11
burger 120–1, 127–8, 220
hollandaise 23–4, 30, 31–2
hot 222
oyster 234
sriracha 48
sweet BBQ 67–8, 76–7, 88–9,
184–5, 203–4, 215
sweet pizza 159–60, 163

tomato
bloody Mary 272
BLT 138
Chicago dog 132–3
chilli 195–6
Cobb salad 112–13
fresh tomato salsa 48, 64,
214
fry bread taco 154–5
garden salad 109
marinara sauce 175–6
nachos 64
for naked chicken burger
122–3
for po' boy 152–3
for smashed burger 120–1
tomato salsa 212–13
tomato sauce 166–8
tomato soup 91, 104–5,
139–40
tomato-chilli sauce 46–7
tuna melt 143
veggie burger patties 127–8
see also tomato ketchup
tomato ketchup 210–11
recipes using 33–4, 42–3, 90,
120–3, 127–30, 148–9,
186–9, 215, 220
tortilla chips 62

accompaniments for 58–61,
64, 196–8, 212, 214
tortillas (corn)
breakfast tacos 48
huevos ranchos 46–7
pizza quesadilla 90
tortilla chips 62
tortillas (wheat flour)
chicken quesadillas 88–9
pizza quesadilla 90
tortilla chips 62
tuna melt 143
turkey, hot turkey sandwich 145

vanilla white icing glaze 262–3,
265
vegetable soup, country 91,
92–3
veggie burger patties 127–8
vodka
bloody Mary 272
penne vodka 171–2

waffles 19–20
Cheddar-bacon 23–4
multi-grain 21–2
strawberry chocolate 268–9,
271
Woolworth, F. W. 1–2